READY OR NOT ...
HERE WE COME!

READY OR NOT...
HERE WE COME!

The REAL Experts'
Cannot-Live-Without Guide
to the First Year With Twins

ELIZABETH LYONS

To order additional copies of this book, contact:
Xlibris Corporation
1-888-795-4274
www.Xlibris.com
Orders@Xlibris.com
18439

CONTENTS

ACKNOWLEDGEMENTS

To Jack and Henry, this book could not have been written without you. For blessing us with your presence, and giving me the opportunity every day to become a more patient, giving, positive person, I will forever be grateful. Just thinking of you makes my heart smile. Jack, you have been on a mission since *before* Day 1. Be sure to slow down and enjoy the scenery every once in awhile! Henry, you are not fooling anyone; your eyes say it all.

To Grace, your ability to adapt to confusing and otherwise crazy situations will serve you well for all your life. You light up every corner of my world. Thank you for never ceasing to make me laugh hysterically, especially during the moments I need to most.

To David, thank you for wrapping my hands in ice and keeping the hospital room at fifty degrees while I suffered through the Magnesium Sulfate days, coordinating our entire lives while I was incarcerated in the hospital, muddling through nighttime feedings before schlepping off to work everyday, and continuing to support every crazy idea I have and every decision I make (well, almost). I love you.

To Dr. Bob Covert, words cannot express how highly I think of you—both as a neonatologist and a person. You have a God-given gift to care for sick babies (and their parents) in the most compassionate and respectable way each and every day. I am so grateful that my children were in your care. You are the most humble physician I have ever met, and you will never know how much we appreciated your friendly, yet candid opinions on whether to stop the drugs, start the drugs, deliver the babies, or continue to will them to stay inside a little bit longer. We will never be able to repay the peace you instilled in us regarding our decisions.

To all of the NICU nurses at Edward Hospital in Naperville, Illinois, thank you for looking after the babies in your care as though they were your own. You are some of the most compassionate, tireless people I have ever met. It is so comforting to parents to know that they can run home to shower or get a bite to eat without feeling anxious because they know their children are in your caring, competent hands.

To all of the Labor and Delivery nurses at Edward Hospital in Naperville, Illinois, specifically Grace, Jean, Nancy Jean, Lynn, Geri, Nancy, Donna, Pat, Ann Marie, Melissa, and Laura, I know I was not the best patient, and I will never forget your kindness, patience, and care. You each give new definition to the term "patient advocate." You are the best of the best.

To Kathy Voit, thank you for tirelessly supporting my plight while I was in the hospital and for all the Starbucks chats since. Your assistance and friendship have been invaluable.

To Debbie Larson in the perinatology clinic, thank you for always being in the best mood and having the greatest laugh!

To Jean Dwyer, thank you for showing up in the delivery room (again!).

To Rian Branch, Tracy Kunce, and Gretchen Keane, I've said it before and I'll say it again—you are angels in Jack and Henry's lives (and many days, mine as well). You will never know how lucky I feel to have the boys in your care. Thank you for your friendship, your patience, your positive attitudes, your fantastic personalities, and for being unbelievably great with kids (not all therapists are, you know!). And thank you for solidifying in my mind the next path that my professional life will (hopefully) take.

To Dr. Kristine Liberty, thank you for your contributions to this book. Thank you for being so knowledgeable and so patient.

To all of the other doctors and nurses at Pediatric Health Associates, thank you for always returning my calls quickly, listening to me ramble on occasion about symptoms before getting to the actual *point* of my call, and, while you probably think it with frequency, thank you for never saying, "Liz, please find another pediatric group. You call *way* too much!"

To Mom, thank you for moving in for five weeks. Thank you for going along with Grace's need to water the vegetable garden at 6:30AM, ensuring that she had a fabulous fall jacket (and some turtlenecks), piggybacking her to my hospital room every day, feeding my husband a great dinner every night, painting my toenails (even though I couldn't see them), and bearing with the discomfort I *know* your back was in through it all. Neither Grace nor I will ever be able to thank you enough. And thank you for editing me (as always).

To Dad, thank you for introducing me to the value of chocolate (and other sugar-loaded treats) at an early age. And thanks for surviving on ice cream and potato chips for those five weeks mom was here and never complaining (though somehow, I doubt you minded the meal selection all that much!).

To Katie Wahn, thank you for designing and creating my website, book cover, postcards, and everything. Thank you for putting up with my lack of knowledge and endless questions (and endless changes). You are a great sister and a better friend. I am so blessed to have you in my life.

To Sharon Auberle, thank you for encouraging me to consider myself a writer, even before I had anything published.

To Stephanie and Kevin Breemes, thank you for coming into our lives when you did, and for taking such good care of any or all of our kids when I needed some help. I could not have done it without you!

To Jenny Commins, thank you ever so much for thinking quickly on your feet, encouraging me to be more daring than I ever thought I could, and making me laugh hysterically in the process. And thank you for "staying you" all of these years! Stay calm, and keep the faith.

To Krisi Monsivaiz, thank you for being a great role model.

You are one of the most amazing people I have ever known, and I'm so fortunate to have you for a friend.

To Karen Summers ("Kara") from Zano Salon in Naperville, Illinois, thank you for making the few haircuts I have time to get such relaxing experiences. Thank you for spending extra time styling the "do" the day the photo for this book was taken!

To Mollie, what on earth would I do without you? I thank the universe every single day for allowing you to get pregnant with twins while on birth control. Thank you for being supportive all the time, and for telling it like it is when necessary.

To Barb, we were most definitely each other's twin in a prior life. Thank you for the sanity-saving phone chats while we were in the hospital (even though we got in "trouble" for having them). And thanks for . . . well . . . everything since! I can't imagine my world without you in it.

Finally, thank you from the very bottom of my heart and pit of my soul to all my other girlfriends in this adventure: Sonya, Holly, Betty, Allison, and Jean. I was meant to travel this "multiples road" with you, I am sure. Thank you for keeping a smile on my face every single day. I am so blessed to have each of you in my life, and my children are as blessed to have you and your children in theirs. When we are eighty years old, I expect to still be trying to coordinate dates for our nights out. I love you all.

A YEAR IN A DAY...

The alarm goes off—in the form of a cry from one of your two new bundles of joy. You look at the clock, and realize it's only been thirty minutes since you last got into bed. You drag your body, which is so tired it feels like a sack of lead, out of bed to feed the screaming baby and change his diaper, possibly twice. Uh oh, another baby is crying. Make her bottle, put her next to you in a bouncy seat, and prop the bottle with the closest stuffed animal you can find so you can finish changing the first baby. Put the baby you just changed back to bed, finish feeding the second baby, and run to use the bathroom before your bladder explodes, and you have to go back to the hospital again!

Stop to momentarily contemplate how relaxing a hospital stay might be at this point.

Crawl back into bed. Close your eyes. Seemingly right away, your eyes shoot open to the sound of a baby crying—again. Look over to your husband's side of the bed. It's empty.

"Good," you think, "he's got him!"

But that baby keeps crying! It's then that you realize that your husband is feeding one baby, but the *other* one is now up. Crawl back into the nursery to check the feeding log to determine if she could *possibly* be hungry *again*. Alright, where did you last leave the feeding log? Crawl under the crib, peek under the changing table. There it is! Deduce that she *could* be hungry. Make a bottle. Approach the crib, ready to supply sustenance to one of your new little angels. But alas, she's sound asleep again. Frown at your husband who only has enough energy to shrug his shoulders in disbelief.

Shuffle back to bed.

Roll out of bed again a bit later to "start the day." Attempt to do two weeks' worth of laundry, and have breakfast in the form of a handful of M&Ms before the babies need to eat again.

Feed. Burp. Change. Repeat.

Check the clock, note that it's 5:00PM, you're still in your pajamas (the same ones you've been wearing for two days), and you haven't showered for three days. Call a friend in a panic because you are sure you won't make it through the next ten minutes. Silently thank God for her as she tells you what a great job you're doing, and then attempts to bring you back to your once sane and rational self by reminding you that she knows you can do this. Thank her, inform her that you are concerned about her judgment, and beg her to come over for a bit because you simply can't handle the thought of making one more bottle.

Nighttime falls. Again and again.

Wake up. Listen intently. Realize you hear nothing but silence and you've been asleep for a solid eight hours. Oh, the joy. Get out of bed. Shower. Put on your pre-pregnancy pants, and style your hair. Pop downstairs for a quick breakfast. Listen to the babies talking to each other in their beds. Walk upstairs, open their door, and watch them jump up, eager to see you and start the day. Take them to the kitchen, and begin that schedule that you have so masterfully crafted.

Deal with a tantrum.

Comfort a sick baby.

Be the proverbial fly on the wall as you watch the greatest friendship of all time develop.

Crawl into bed.

Sleep all night . . . again.

And dream of the amazing life only a mother of twins knows.

WHY I WROTE THIS BOOK

W elcome to the adventure! And an adventure it will be, I
promise. At some point during the middle of one of our
longer nights with our newborn twin boys, Jack and Henry, I sat
on the floor—no doubt in the same pajamas I had been wearing
for four days or more—and thought to myself, There really should
be an operations manual for these guys! (And I already had a two
year old!) While I was pregnant with my sons, I found some
wonderful books on the medical aspects of a twin pregnancy and
the basic logistics of surviving that all-important and hectic first
year, but none that addressed the whole event in a true girlfriend-
to-girlfriend manner. I didn't want anyone to unnecessarily
sugarcoat it. I wanted someone to be honest and say, "Honey,
raising twins is hard!" Most of the books out there do that. What
frustrated me about those books was that after telling me it was
hard, I wanted them to say, "Here's how you make it easier (and
laugh while you're doing it)." The few that did gave only one or
two solutions—solutions that often did not work for my kids—
and they did not inspire laughter! I longed for a humorous book
that would tell it like it is and also give a variety of strategies for
getting through the "how it is." It was at that point that I decided
to write this.

As for A Year in a Day—I'm only just starting year two, but I
have no doubt (and I've confirmed it with my girlfriends in the
event that I'm momentarily losing my mind) that this is a relatively

accurate overall illustration of the first year with twins. It's crazy, and it's amazing, and it goes by all too quickly. What initially does not seem survivable some days will have you laughing hysterically as you think back. Just wait. Occasionally, I'll see a new mom of twins and I can't help but say, "Congratulations—it's going to be the best time you've ever had." Some of these women smile and say, "Thanks," some look at me like I'm crazy (I'm sure it's just the painkillers still in their systems), and some say, "Really? I hope so!" I think moms of twins are too often told (frequently by people who have no experience with twins) how hard the journey is going to be, and I think that's terribly sad. I mean, of *course* it will be hard—but some days, picking up one's dry cleaning on time is hard. The difference is that this experience will be the most rewarding kind of "hard" you'll ever face.

It's true that I am writing as a stay-at-home mom (as I always say, "I work, I just don't get paid in currency"), however, what I have to say can be just as valuable to working moms. After all, *someone* has to know how to run your house, whether it's you or your husband or your nanny! Several of my girlfriends who have twins work full-time, and several of the strategies presented throughout this book are theirs.

Being a mother of twins is one of the most amazing experiences around. Being a mom period is amazing, but to bring two children into the world simultaneously, raise them as their own unique selves, and watch as they grow and develop into the people they were meant to be is simply astonishing. It's a hard road, but nothing worthwhile is ever easy, right? And so much of it is in your perspective and your attitude. There will be days, of course, when you think, Screw attitude and perspective, this sucks! But those days will be few and far between and you will get past them, I promise. People will comment that God never gives you more than you can handle, and you will think, Yes, but unfortunately, He's confused me with someone else. And then, that baby you've been hoping would sleep for more than six minutes at a time will sleep for an hour. You will know you were meant to mother these babies. You will discover parts of your brain and parts of your heart that you never knew existed. The universe does know what it's doing when it sends two babies with one stork. Parents may not know why they were chosen, and at times may feel as if they have no idea what they are doing, but that stork is smiling all the way back to heaven.

When I first started writing this book, I wanted to include a section at the beginning of each chapter that would focus on what had made that particular phase work. I gave a lot of thought to this concept, but I was never entirely confident in my conclusions. They felt forced. One day, when the boys were thirteen months old and Grace was three, we were in the process of moving to a new house. Jack was scaling the now-unprotected fireplace, Henry was screaming because Jack was doing something "bad," Grace was running around pretending to paint the walls with about one hundred Swiffer cloths, and some unsuspecting potential buyers were coming through the front door amidst the chaos. (We hadn't yet sold the old house when we were forced to close on the new one.) It was at this point that the "what" of what makes it all work suddenly dawned on me. It's two things: faith and perspective. You must have faith in yourself, your spouse, your friends, your family, the universe, God, some other higher power, chocolate—whatever makes you feel confident and capable. (I believe that the power of chocolate is often *highly* underrated!) You simply must have faith that you were chosen to mother these babies for a reason; that you will make it through; that everything happens for a reason; and that it's all just one big test you are going to pass with flying colors. Perhaps not every day, mind you, but at the end of the race, you will have succeeded.

The right perspective is just as important. Somewhat surprisingly, I meet other mothers of twins left and right. Many of their kids are older now and they comment on how it gets more fun every year. Only about one percent of all the women I've talked with say something stupid like, "Oh, it only gets harder as they get older." I've never understood that. Even if that *were* their perspective, what benefit does it provide to tell me that? One mom I met summed it up perfectly. She said, "People without twins make such a big deal out of *how* you do it. You just do it! You have a sense of humor about it as often as possible. And you take it a day, sometimes an hour, at a time."

You must realign your expectations from the beginning. If you are a person who needs your house to be spotless day-in and day-out, you will need to invent (and quickly) some sort of twelve-step program for yourself to slowly break your need to have the house completely clean all the time. In fact, I seem to remember an evening when David walked into the house, having just arrived home from work. I was sweating, unshowered, hungry, and unable to find Jack's pajamas that I had *just* set out. Poor guy mentioned something about a major sale on some speakers he's waited years to buy and my retort was simple and straightforward. I said, through clenched teeth, "Money does not grow on trees and neither do housekeepers. Look at this place! Now give me some *help!*" I think he was actually scared because he didn't waste a lot of time going for the vacuum cleaner. Whether it was my appearance or my demeanor he was so afraid of, I'm not entirely sure.

You will need to accept that unless you can hire a personal chef, you will probably not dine on a gourmet meal every night. In fact, most nights still, a bowl of cereal sounds just delicious and, as I will mention again later, I rely heavily on the power of the multi-vitamin!

I am slowly accepting that this year, my holiday cards may not go out until March. As my husband frequently comments, "There are not enough hours in the day or adults in this house!" If you allow it, you will have "to do" lists seven miles long—and that's OK, provided you train yourself to be able to prioritize three or four "to do's" in a *week* instead of in a *day* as might have been your practice in the past.

I had the unbelievable good fortune of meeting seven amazing women through a multiples birthing class at our local hospital. We hit it off as though we had known each other in some prior life. We went through our pregnancies, our bed rests, our hospitalizations, and now continue to go through our parenting together. The hospital staff still marvels at our group, often referring to it as the "multiples sorority," because even though a multiples class is offered quarterly at the hospital, no group has ever bonded the way we did. There was a point at which four or five of us were all in the hospital on large amounts of drugs to stop pre-term labor, and after we had sent our husbands to the snack room for yet another Sprite and cranberry juice concoction, we wondered where they were when they didn't return after twenty or thirty minutes. Turns out, they were each in the hall with the other husbands, talking football or basketball or dilation. They get along as well as we do. That support was provided for each of us early on, possibly because God didn't think any of us would make it through without one another. Many days, I think He was right. Trust that the universe will provide you with what (or whom) you need to make this work.

I should also probably note at this point that in the early weeks, our families helped a lot, but the reality was that they all lived hundreds of miles away and couldn't take up permanent residence with us. I've purchased books about how to get through challenging times only to find on page 12 that the survivor of said times had two nannies, a plethora of family members living nearby, and a bottomless bank account. None of those applied to us. My neighbors were kind enough to bring dinner four nights in a row, and I truly believe that the only thing that kept several of my friends who live in other states from getting on planes and coming to help was their responsibility to their own children.

On a particularly challenging morning, I received a "just checking in" phone call from my girlfriend Barb. I met Barb in the multiples class I mentioned earlier and ever so slowly, our lives began imitating each other's. Barb got put on bed rest; the next day I got put on bed rest. I went into the hospital in pre-term labor; two days later Barb was right across the hall with her own Magnesium Sulfate drip. Barb's contractions got too frequent and she had to have *more* Magnesium Sulfate. Three hours later, so did I. So, when I arrived to actually deliver the babies, I told the nursing staff that they might as well set up the second delivery room while they were at it because I expected Barb to show up any minute. As it turned out, she had her girls nine days after Jack and Henry were born.

When Barb called that particular morning, we could barely hear each other for all the heck breaking loose in the background of my happy home. The boys were screaming uncontrollably; I had no idea what was wrong with them. I had been feeding them practically around the clock, and knew that they were probably tired, but while I tried to convince them that it would be easier to fall asleep if they would stop screaming, they didn't seem to believe me. I was sitting Indian-style on a loveseat with Jack on one knee and Henry on the other, trying to feed them simultaneously from bottles (and it was not going well). Barb said, "I'll tell you what. My mother-in-law is here. Why don't I come over and give you a hand." I said, "*What?* No. You have two babies of your own over there. I'll be just fine (I think)." She told me to call at any time if I passed the point of no return, and she would come right over. I thanked her, hung up, and went back to my attempt to comfort the babies. (I have no memory of where Grace was during this time.) A few minutes later, I heard a tap on the door. Oh, this ought to be good, I thought. I cannot get up, I have not showered in days, and there is intense screaming going on in here! I peeked around to see Barb looking in through the sidelights of our front door. I could not believe it (though knowing her as I do now, I can). I managed to get up and open the door and she just said, "I knew you would not call." She came in, looked around, and said, "Now, what exactly is the problem here?" You see, the moment Barb walked in the door, both boys stopped crying. The only thing that saved me from being seen as a complete drama queen in need of major attention was that she had heard the decibel level of their screaming when she called earlier. Barb stayed for about thirty minutes (the boys did not make so much as a peep while she was here), walked out the front door, and the screaming began again. Still clueless, I prepared two more bottles, thanked the gods of true friendship, and said a silent prayer to those of calm and quiet. To this day, Barb still provides those momentary miracles in my life, and I am so thankful each and every time.

It is important to go into this adventure with your eyes wide open. It will be a challenge. It is important to go into it knowing you will have good days and not-so-good days. It is most important to have respect for how lucky you are. Many mothers of multiples did not get there by sheer coincidence (unless you are my girlfriend Mollie and conceived fraternal twins while on birth control, but she's a unique individual). Many of us tried and tried and had to resort to whatever methods were available to be able to carry a child. We didn't get too picky about how many we had to carry at once just so long as we got the opportunity to become a mother. So, it rarely dawns on us to complain (well, too much) or wonder *how* we are going to do it. Like that other mom said, we just do it. You remind yourself that the challenging times are going to be infrequent compared with the joys, the triumphs, and the miracles that you will experience as a mother of twins. In your darkest, most sleep-deprived moments, you must force yourself to remember that it could be worse. And if you can't convince yourself of that fact, just pick up the paper or turn on the world news. That should confirm it almost immediately!

In order to raise my kids full-time, I've given up a career and with it, some friends. I've temporarily given up variety in my life (outside the variety that occurs each day in my crazy home), the ability to pick up and travel on a moment's notice, the practice of eating three solid meals a day that consist of more than Rice Krispies or Nutri-Grain bars, and that's just for starters. And I have never been happier in all my life. There are some tough hours and some tough days. But the rewards are so much greater than anything I could ever have imagined. I watch my daughter get excited about doing a Santa Claus box for a needy child somewhere else in the world. I watch as Henry crawls faster and faster even though he's relatively late achieving this milestone. I watch as Jack develops his sweet, yet mischievous personality. Even though no one else seems to know it (or care), I know I am far more capable of controlling corporate chaos than some of the world's most esteemed corporate leaders. After all, if you have multiples, you can multi-task with much greater skill than the best of them. My days are crazy and my nights are way too short, but my life has more meaning than ever.

You have been truly blessed. Twins are given to those who can survive the task of raising them and who will know unconditionally underneath it all what a blessing they have been given. That is precisely why mothers of twins have no idea what that lady in the grocery store is talking about when she cocks her head to the side and with puppy-dog eyes informs you how sorry she feels for you.

Keep your sense of humor. If you don't have one, get one—FAST! Find the beauty in the not-so-great moments. A poignant example: I remember when I was miserable in my hospital bed, having been there for a full week already just after the September 11 attacks, on a multitude of drugs to prevent delivering my boys too early, missing my daughter, and trying to locate my parents who were stuck in Europe. Our friend Betty was in hard labor with her twins (she had made it to thirty-nine weeks!) when an OB nurse wheeled her into my room in her bed. I said, "Um, should you not be in the delivery room about now?" As I looked more closely (Magnesium Sulfate will render you nearly blind), I saw that she was holding her son Collin in one arm and her daughter Morgan in the other. I just cried. More than once, you will be at what feels like your lowest point and then the Betty in your life will be wheeled in. Well, maybe not Betty exactly, though she is pregnant again "by surprise" and the twins are just over a year old, so if you live in the area and spend any time in the hospital in pre-term labor, who knows, it may actually be Betty who's wheeled in with her newest bundle of joy! But the very thing that the story of Betty represents will occur. You will be presented with something that makes your heart soar, makes you forget the challenge and be so grateful for having this amazing opportunity.

The sorority sisters and I have been living this whirlwind together for a year now. We've all had our up and our down moments. We've all had challenges, and we've all found solutions. I hope with all of my heart that one of the many solutions we've utilized—often invented on-the-fly—will benefit you. I wish you as many amazing, tear-jerking moments as I have experienced. I wish you supportive friends and family, restful nights, and late-starting mornings. And, of course, a cupboard full of chocolate.

TOP TEN SECRETS TO SURVIVING THE FIRST YEAR

10. Constantly remind yourself that you *will* sleep again. You will again eat a full meal while it is still warm. You will again change out of your pajamas before 3:00 in the afternoon.

9. Accept that you will make mistakes. Promise yourself that you will do the best you can, and that when a strategy does not work, you will fall back, regroup, and try again.

8. Promise your spouse that you will share your feelings, positive or negative, about the whole experience.

7. Set aside some time for yourself each day—even if it is only ten minutes—to take a long, relaxing bath or shower. As the babies get older, take some time to get out of the house and/or be with friends as often as possible.

6. Remember how blessed you are, even when you haven't been granted a good night's sleep in weeks or a good meal in days. Remember that it could always be worse (really, it could!).

5. Find the humor in as much of the not-so-fun stuff as you can. Sometimes, all you can do is laugh or cry, and the former is much more fun.

4. When you need to cry, cry.

3. Trust yourself and your instincts no matter what. You were chosen to mother these babies for a reason.

2. Although it may be against your nature, allow yourself to lean

on people. You will have many years to repay their kindness and you will add these moments of thoughtfulness to those you cherish along with all the other special memories of this first year. Let your neighbor pick up some much-needed groceries or a prescription if she is headed that way, or ask a friend to help you take your children to their doctor's appointment. As my friend Holly (who really had trouble letting people help her) commented, "Even with a poor postpartum memory, I remember every person who sent a meal or watched the kids so my husband and I could step out. Those memories are forever with me and I am so thankful for every one."

1. Keep the cupboards stocked with chocolate (or whatever other indulgence makes you happy) and splurge on a lottery ticket at least once every two months—you never know!

<u>ONE</u>

Anticipating the Storks:
The Father's Side

By Bob Evanosky

L isten up, guys! Here's the crash course on fathering twins in the first year.

When Liz asked me to write this section, my first question was, "When?" I carved out time because the truth is that I have a great perspective from which to write. I have spent half of my sons' lives as the primary breadwinner and half as the primary caretaker. I have seen it from both sides and frankly, while there are days when I'm not sure which angle is better, I would not trade any of it for even a second.

Let me start by saying one thing: Women are amazing. Men simply could not endure what women go through to bring these babies into the world. When our boys were born on November 5, by Cesarean Section, I looked down and saw Sonya's uterus on her stomach. At that moment, I thought to myself, "*Geez*, they have her uterus on the outside of her body. This is wild!" Then, I thought, "Thank God she's the one with the uterus because you would *not* get me to do this!"

The biggest hurdle in this game of fathering multiples is the high learning curve—one that you must master quickly and, often, on-the-fly. What we must be thankful for every second is the fact that women are ten times more prepared than men would ever be for this parenting thing no matter how many babies they are expecting because they are naturally maternal. They educate themselves to the "nth" degree through the Internet, books, support groups, and other women. The man's approach tends to be more of the "I'll deal with it as it comes" kind. We think, "It can't be *that* hard." Men are often more laid back about the details, the how and when of doing everything. Women feel they have the responsibility as mothers to get as much information as possible in order to be the best mothers they can be. In some ways, this discordance in approach is good because it allows one of you to be a little more laid back and relaxed. It can also cause big problems because what may happen is that your wife will begin to feel as though you are not really interested in what is happening to her physically and emotionally during her pregnancy or in the ways your lives are going to change once the babies are born. Your wife may believe that you are assuming she will take care of it all and that may make her feel overwhelmed. Or, she may feel as though you are not as excited or happy as she is or perhaps that you don't really care.

If I were to do it again, I would definitely have been more supportive of Sonya by making certain that I read the same books she read and discussed them with her. It was important to do that because *she* found it of high value. While you may rather pick up the latest copy of *Sports Illustrated* or *In Fisherman*, opt instead for spending some time with your wife reading the stack of pregnancy, childbirth, and child-rearing books that have more than likely accumulated by her side of the bed. Do it in support of her. I found that there were things I took for granted that I would have known had I read what she was reading. Once our boys were born, my wife was frustrated that I didn't know these things. Reading with her would have made everything run much more smoothly.

THE BABIES ARE HERE!

During the 0- to 3-month period, it is critical to remember that women are still recovering from the birth and possibly from bedrest and a difficult pregnancy and/or delivery. Thus, the period of time from birth until the babies are three months old is the most intense period on a number of levels. Many twins spend some time initially in the Neonatal Intensive Care Unit (NICU). The number of days the babies might spend there can vary. It is important during this period to be honest about your feelings, both with yourself and with your wife. Use other parents, if you have them available to you (long-time friends, or perhaps new friends you might have met in a multiples class), for support. Utilize NICU doctors and nurses as well. Be prepared for the various transitional issues your babies might face such as the inability to regulate their body temperatures, undeveloped sucking reflexes, and feeding issues. Understand that transitional issues are often a "one step forward, two steps back" proposition. Ultimately, the babies will be fine, but you have to be patient. Believe me, it is in your best interest to be prepared for these issues up-front. In a way, I was lucky because most of the babies from our multiples class were born a few weeks ahead of ours. I was able to see several of them in the NICU. Our babies didn't have some of the issues others had, so I felt OK about their condition. Had I not seen some of the other babies, I might not have been as strong. It's almost always just a function of time for all the transitional prematurity issues to clear themselves up.

Once the babies are home, Phase Two begins. This phase is all about making it work, minute by minute. It is during this 0- to 3-month time that your wife is really going to need you. We don't always have a huge job in this whole process, but when we're called to the plate, we have to hit a grand slam because that's when our wives badly need us. My biggest piece of advice: Don't come home and ask your wife what she did all day. For the first five months of our sons' lives, Sonya was the primary caregiver. As a pilot, I would often be gone for three to four days at a time and after walking in the front door, without saying it, would think, "What went on here? This is chaos!" After those first five months, I retired from my job to be the primary caregiver, and Sonya went back to work. During my first two weeks at home I thought I was going to shoot myself. About ten days into it, I told myself, "I've made a huge mistake. What have I done? I just resigned from a major airline job that only 50,000 people in the world have, and I walked away from it for *this*!" But what I needed was a realignment of my expectations. Believe me, a man who works nine hours a day or longer has unrealistic expectations of what really goes on at home while he's not there. I know that because I've been on both sides. In those first two weeks as the primary caregiver, I truly had to become a woman. What I couldn't handle, and what put me totally over the edge, was the fact that I had to arrange *my* entire schedule around the boys. I initially thought that I'd be able to force them onto my schedule, but that just did not work. It's fair to say that men can't understand this all-day-with-the-babies lifestyle having not experienced it, but they must admit that they can't understand it, and appreciate that it is hard at the same time. Your wife doesn't get paid, but her job is one of the most important of all. And it never ends! You don't work as hard at any job as you do as the primary caregiver.

As that primary caregiver, my day is solid from 5:30AM to 8:30PM. Few jobs require that. There are some people who might work these hours of their own free will (and they are nuts), but this job requires it. You can't sit down when your kids need to eat. You can't put your kids to bed in pajamas with spit-up formula running down the front of them.

Men who are *not* the primary caregivers cannot assume that when they come home from work their workday is over. They need to change clothes and dive in. Do some laundry, help feed the kids, send your wife out for a walk or a trip to the mall or bookstore—something to give her a break. Reassure her that what she's doing is invaluable. Work with her to understand what she needs to feel good and rejuvenated—perhaps going out alone at night for a few hours to run errands, going for a walk, or getting her hair cut. Many stay-at-home moms quickly begin to feel as though their lives are more or less one-dimensional. There are so many ways you can help with this. After all, they say that having one child changes a woman's world—imagine two!

Finally, amidst the chaos and the awe, never forget in how many amazing, wonderful ways these new babies will change your lives. For every smile you would get with one baby, you will get two with twins. In a matter of seconds, you will add two more special little people to your family and to the world. These babies will depend on you for many years to come and so will your wife. If you step up to that plate with confidence and excitement, you will surely hit that grand slam!

TWO

Before the Arrivals:

Preparing the Lair

D o We Really Need Two of Everything? This was one of the first questions my husband and I asked ourselves—and we already had one of almost everything! The answer is: Yes and no. Here's the lowdown.

BABIES' GEAR

There is no doubt about it—when you have a baby, you need a lot of gear. When you have two babies at once, you need even *more* gear! The good news is that beyond clothing and diapers, it's not as much more as you might expect.

I definitely believe in getting as much life out of items as possible, so I recommend being forward-thinking when choosing the gear for the nursery. Some cribs can be converted to toddler beds or full-size beds, and some rocking chairs have more flexibility in terms of future use than others. As if you don't have enough to think about, try to think long-term when picking out these items. In two or three years, you will be quite thankful that you did.

Now, a quick word about new versus used gear. There is absolutely nothing on earth wrong with borrowing as many pieces of equipment as possible, or buying them in gently used condition from garage sales, resale shops, or friends. You will not believe for how short a period of time the items will be used. Plus, the amount of money you can save by borrowing or buying gently used equipment could quite conceivably fund about fifty percent of one of the babies' college educations. However, a few precautions should be taken with this approach. The one item I do not recommend buying used, unless you know and are very comfortable with the previous owner, is a car seat. You just have no way of knowing if it was ever in an accident, and technically, car seats should not be used once they have been involved in an accident, even if it was only a fender-bender. These days, most insurance companies cover the cost of a new car seat if a car has been involved in a fender-bender of any magnitude.

Additionally, any time you purchase something from a garage sale, resale shop, or even one of your closest friends, do a check on www.cpsc.gov to ensure that the item has not been recalled. Sometimes, if it has, you can order the part that will render the item completely safe. Other times, it might be better to simply look around for another product that appears more reliable. After all, this is very precious cargo we're dealing with here!

If you are lucky enough to receive two of absolutely everything at a shower, or a combination of showers, well then high-five sister! A word of advice: Don't put everything together right away. Put together only those things you are sure you will use, and keep the others (the second swing, second exersaucer, and so forth) aside. If you end up needing them, great. If not, items advertised as New With Tags (NWT) or New In Box (NIB) go like hotcakes on eBay. Trust me, you can always use a few dollars to pay for that second pair of shoes or the fantastic outfits from the boutique that you can neither live without nor afford. And by all means, keep the original packing boxes if you have the space. They will come in handy later when you go to sell all this gear. (More on the eBay project later.)

Cribs

You will ultimately need two cribs. The babies can certainly co-sleep in the beginning should you choose to have them do so, but ultimately, they will be big enough that they will need to have their own cribs in order to be safe (and have room to move around). If you plan to have your babies co-sleep for the first few months, you do not need to purchase two cribs right away. We purchased our second crib after the babies were born, and waited to assemble it until the boys were at a point when we knew they would soon need to be separated.

Changing Table

I truly believe that a changing table is an optional piece of equipment. It's convenient at first, and most times, you can buy one that coordinates with the crib. Honestly though, I would be surprised if you were using it too much after the first few weeks. To carry one baby upstairs every time he needs a new diaper gets tiring, and to have to do that with two babies is beyond tiring—in fact, it's absurd! Several of my friends bought a changing table and kept it downstairs so that they had a convenient place to store all of the diaper-changing supplies and change the babies but did not have to hike up fourteen steps to do it. Another idea, if you simply must have a changing table, is to get the kind that is a dresser underneath with a diaper-changing attachment on the top. This way, whenever you decide that you've had it with hiking upstairs to change diapers, you simply remove the diaper-changing piece and fancy that—you have a dresser! Then, you won't feel the guilt that comes with eliminating an entire piece of basically new furniture.

Rocking Chair or Glider

I believe that this is another optional piece of equipment, but a nice-to-have piece as well. It is comfortable and convenient to rock a baby in at 3:00AM. If you get one that is aesthetically versatile, it could conceivably find a spot in your own bedroom or another room of your house once your nursery becomes a big kid's room. Or, if you get the kind that's more of an upholstered rocking armchair, you can have it reupholstered if you desire and leave it in your children's room as a reading chair (or move it to *your* room as a reading chair!).

Car Seats

There is no getting around the fact that you must have two infant car seats. You can either purchase the kind that snaps into the base in the car and has a handle by which to carry it, or the kind that converts from an infant seat to a toddler seat to a booster seat and stays in your car on a permanent basis. Let me make this decision very easy for you. Get the seats that snap into the seat base and allow you to carry the babies in them. They are convenient, especially to snap into the stroller for those trips out, even though— because you are carrying two of them—they will get heavier and heavier earlier than just one. Now, my girlfriend Mollie kept her boys in their infant car seats until they were nearly ten months old and about seventeen pounds each, but her biceps are probably firmer than mine at this point.

Ensure that the car seats fit into your car properly, and attend a car seat check or make an appointment at your local police station to ensure that the bases are installed properly. This takes very little time and provides great peace of mind. Most police stations have officers who will do this for you free of charge and I assure you, once they get them in, they are *not* coming loose. When we got the boys' infant seats installed, two 250-pound officers both had a knee in each seat, pushing it down. Both were sweating profusely. They want those seats to be as tight and as safe as possible. Another option is to check for car seat inspections done locally. Babies "R" Us usually offers them every quarter or so, and they are done by folks who know exactly how those car seats should fit in there. Many police stations offer publicized inspections on occasion as well.

If your babies spend any time in the NICU, a nurse from that unit will most likely do a car seat check before you are able to leave. This means that the nurse will put each baby in his car seat and monitor his breathing for about an hour to ensure that he is positioned properly to avoid having difficulty breathing. This test will be inconvenient if you have to take the larger convertible car seats out of your car, haul them inside for the test, and then reinstall them. It is far easier to have the infant seats that you can just take in with you (another great reason to invest in the infant seats instead of the convertible seats). Also, some babies are so small even when they go home that the convertible models just won't work. The babies need to be secure and have the straps fit appropriately on their little bodies.

Swings

If you are lucky enough to receive two swings as gifts, by all means, accept them! If not, buy or borrow one and wait to see if you will need another. Frequently, one baby loves the swing and the other hates it. Or, one loves it on Monday, Wednesday, and Friday, and the other wants it Tuesday, Thursday, Saturday, and every other Sunday. They take up enough space in your house (no matter how big your house might be) that it makes sense to determine if you will actually need two before cluttering your home any more than is already the case. I will never forget seeing pictures of my girlfriend Holly's house, all ready for her triplets, with three swings, three bouncy seats, three highchairs, and two, if not three, exersaucers all lined up throughout the kitchen and family room. My first thought was, Holly, these girls are not going to crawl *out* of your uterus and *into* the exersaucer. But she was just getting prepared, which, if I haven't mentioned it before, is Holly's middle name. She must also have some sort of psychic abilities because as it turned out, all three girls loved just about everything, and I think she actually needed it all!

I found myself sprinting to Target one evening just before they closed because I finally had to acknowledge that despite the fact that my family room had become a virtual obstacle course, I *had* to have two swings. My boys loved them. So, I lucked out and was able to get one without 600 bells and whistles at a reasonable price (I mean really, they only want to swing in the thing, not learn the alphabet and the words to seventy-five songs while they are in there). The pattern even matched my family room décor perfectly. Imagine that! If you realize that you need two, ask around and see if any friends who have older kids still have a swing that you could borrow (and one that has not been recalled or that you would be afraid to put a small puppet in for fear of it falling apart instantaneously). To my great chagrin, almost everyone I knew had borrowed hers from someone else. Most people in the world are, I suppose, more economical than I am—or, I should say, than I *was*. I have always preferred new things, in the box, with the instructions and the fabric in perfect, untouched condition. That is, until there were *two* little people to buy for.

Bouncy Seats

You are definitely going to need two of these. In fact, if you get really lucky at garage sales or have a lot of generous friends, opt for four. I know several people who kept two upstairs and two downstairs so that when they wanted to go upstairs and take a shower, fold laundry, or just lie on their bed still in PJs at 4:00 in the afternoon, they had seats right there to put the babies into without having to lug them upstairs. Plugging those children into the bouncies, pushing "Play" on the Baby Mozart video, and climbing into bed can make for the most enjoyable hour of the day.

The only great controversy I am aware of with regard to bouncy seats is whether to vibrate or not to vibrate. When our daughter,

Grace, was born, the vibrating bouncy seats had just come on the market. My friend Keena's husband would positively not allow her to get one for their newborn son because he was afraid that the vibration would render the child sterile. I laughed, thought about it for six seconds, and laughed again. I do not believe that any pediatricians are strongly considering this possibility, but if it concerns you, by all means check with your doctor. I used the vibrating seat for Jack and Henry and am just crossing my fingers that one day, they will indeed be able to provide us with grandchildren, should that be their choice.

Front-pack Carriers

Front-pack carriers are wonderful for several reasons. First, they allow you to carry one baby hands-free when necessary, such as in grocery stores. Second, they allow you to carry a baby who simply *has* to be held, and keep your hands free to do something else at the same time, such as eat! The sorority's favorite carrier is made by Baby Bjorn, but there are plenty of other companies that make carriers with which new mothers have found success. In my experience, the only downside to front-pack carriers is that babies cannot safely be held in them until they reach approximately eight pounds. If you are like me, you will be holding each baby on the scale with you several times a day when you know he or she is nearing the eight-pound mark, and when the reading on the scale finally reaches your weight plus eight pounds, you will be so pleased that you will put that carrier on and carry that baby around in it for no other reason than because you can! Some Internet sites that sell products designed for multiples carry infant front-pack carriers that can accommodate two or three babies. This is a neat concept, but once the babies reach more than about eight pounds each, you will avoid using the contraption at all costs because it will simply be too heavy. Also, when I need a good laugh, I envision both babies strapped onto me in a double front-pack carrier and the moment it becomes clear I need to get one of them out (in a hurry). I imagine myself playing an upright version of one-man Twister in an attempt to accomplish such a feat. If you think that such a contraption might benefit you, by all means, give it a try. But don't say I didn't warn you!

Strollers

Stroller selection is one of many topics for which I have great passion. I am known in small circles as "The Stroller Queen." Why? Because I own *way* too many strollers. With my daughter, I would buy a stroller and then find an outing for which that thing just did not work. Therefore, I would acquire another stroller, and on it went until I had four or five—for one child. Needless to say, when I got pregnant with the boys and the topic of a new stroller came up, David said, "One. You get ONE new stroller, so make your choice wisely." And I did. Or so I thought.

I really gave this great mind-time. What would I do most with the kids? What would I *not* do with the kids? I decided that mostly, I would like to run with them in the evenings, take long walks outside, and maybe take them to a park on the weekend that would have rocky pathways and require solid wheels. I determined up-front that the activity I would *not* do was take the babies shopping. I would positively not even entertain the idea of taking all three of my kids shopping. So, after all that thought and some research, I bought a double jogging stroller. Love it. It's great for walks. It's great for the zoo and other outdoor outings. But I have never run with it. And the number of times I've taken all three of my kids to the mall would astound you because it astounds me. However, it's all about survival, and in the middle of winter when you have been pretty much housebound for nearly six months, the image you concoct of yourself strolling through the local mall strongly resembles one of you walking through the shopping area of the Atlantis Hotel in the Bahamas.

I don't know about your local malls, but most of the stores in mine do not accommodate a double jogging stroller (or any kind of side-by-side double stroller). Most of them, specifically the baby stores, barely accommodate a single stroller (a fact that I've always found incredibly odd, but is a topic for another book entirely).

When the boys were about nine months old, I bought a front-back double stroller. It was one of the greatest purchases I ever made and I have not regretted it for a second. My husband almost left me when he saw it in the garage, but seeing the happiness this new stroller has instilled in me has made it all worth it, I'm sure.

The bottom line on strollers is: Go with your gut and be prepared for the fact that your gut may be wrong. In fact, come to think of it, that is a brilliant piece of advice for this entire twin thing! Side-by-side double strollers are tricky to push through doors, and just the sheer width of them alone makes them difficult to navigate, especially in a confined space. Double jogging strollers are fantastic if you do run (or even if you have great intentions, like I did), and are wonderful for walks and other outdoor excursions. They are not great for malls or other stores, however, and a video of me trying to get double doors open to get it into the store in the first place could win awards on *America's Funniest Videos.*

There are front-back double strollers that accommodate infant car seats. Of those, some have a stadium-seating arrangement so that the kid in back can see over the kid in front. A downside of this style is that usually, the back seat only reclines halfway because the strollers are made with the toddler/new baby structure in mind. That's the kind I bought, but it worked because I didn't get it until the boys were much older and didn't need to be fully reclined. There are also true twin front-back double strollers where both the front and back seats fully recline and both seats usually accept infant car seats. The only disadvantage to this type of stroller is that if you have two children who have to be able to see what is in front of them at all times, you'll have an angry baby at some point because, without the stadium seating, she will only be able to stare at her sibling's head!

If you have friends with two children, talk with them about what has worked in their situation. Go look at strollers and think about how you are most likely to use the stroller (and I can guarantee that shopping, whether you think so now or not, will make up a *huge* number of those activities). Most important, as with everything else during this first year, be ready to have made a slight misjudgment. It's OK. You'll figure out what you need, figure out how to get it, and move on.

Pack 'n Plays

Pack 'n Plays are a great investment. However, they are not small. I would definitely recommend getting at least one of these, but if you aren't given two, I would hold off on the second one just in case you don't need it. The only time I can think of when you would definitely need two is if you go on a trip and need one for each baby to sleep in. If this is the only time you need a second one, consider borrowing it from a friend instead of making the double investment just for those outings. I own two, but merely because I borrowed one of my girlfriend Barb's and then proceeded to open the trunk of my very stylish, I'm-a-mom minivan only to have it come crashing out and tear. So, I bought her a new one and now own the one with the torn cover that is an absolute beast to assemble. I'm completely confident that it is not going to crash even with Jack jumping in it because it's been stuck in the upright position for weeks at a time; no one can figure out how to break it down!

The Pack 'n Plays with the built-in changing table and bassinet are especially handy to have around for those first few months. Both babies can nap together in your family room (but only for a little while, then it's time to teach them to sleep in their cribs! More on that later.) These days, several models also come with mobiles, music, and/or vibration. You never know what these kids are going to like, so just go with whatever you feel is the cutest and most functional. And whether you are buying it yourself or putting it on a registry (and praying someone else will buy it) will most likely guide your decision on how fancy it needs to be.

Highchairs

Since having my daughter, a wonderful little piece of equipment has come out: the booster seat. Not the kind that can be used only for a toddler, but the kind that reclines and can be used for a baby *or* a toddler. It is basically a highchair that straps to an adult chair so it doesn't take up extra room in your kitchen. Additionally, you can unstrap it and take it to friends' houses when you are going to be there during a meal, which you could not do with those huge highchairs! The First Years makes a booster seat that we have all had huge success with (and enjoyed lining up in a row of about fifteen at our play outings!).

Exersaucers

While still available for purchase, most pediatricians and pediatric physical therapists no longer recommend actual walkers (basically a small exersaucer on wheels). They have been proven to actually delay an infant's physical development—particularly in the areas of sitting, crawling, and walking. There is also concern about babies walking themselves right down a flight of stairs; I did just that when I was nine months old. The US Consumer Product Safety Commission has blamed baby walkers for causing more injuries than any other children's product.

Exersaucers, on the other hand, can be true lifesavers as long as the child does not spend his entire day in it. However, they take up loads of space. The ones with the most bells and whistles are also expensive. So, follow the "gift rule." If you are blessed to receive two, fantastic! Put one together and wait to assemble the other until you absolutely need it. If you don't receive two, purchase one and if your babies are truly fighting over it day in and day out, you can buy or borrow another one. We only had one and since Jack merely wanted to climb in and out of it by nine months of age, Henry was the only one who could safely use it anyway.

Crib Sheets

The final word on crib sheets is this: Have at least two per crib. Three is better. I've heard of some moms who are able to layer crib sheets and mattress pads two or three sets thick so that when the top sheet is dirty, they just pull off the sheet and accompanying mattress pad (that has prevented the layer-two sheet from getting wet) and voilà, you have a freshly made crib. My crib mattress fits into my crib so tightly that it is a ten-minute aerobic workout just to get one mattress pad and sheet on it, so I am forced to re-sheet it each time. But I figure I can always use more exercise.

Mattress Protectors

I learned a key lesson on this one. There is a type of mattress protector that fits more like a pillowcase than a sheet. It's plastic. You slip the mattress into it and zip it up. This way, when you go to put on the sheet—or, more importantly, take it off—the whole mattress pad does not come with it. It is a godsend. I have only seen them at Target, but other stores may carry them. Buy two.

Bathtubs

You truly need only one baby bathtub and you may not even need that, depending on how you end up bathing your babies. (There is a whole section on bathing in the 0-3 Month chapter, so skip ahead to that for suggestions if you would like.) You don't need a lot of "extras" with the bathtub, but a drain spout as well as slots to hold shampoo, washcloths, and a rinsing cup are nice. The baby bathtubs are inexpensive, so it's wise to get one, but you definitely will not need two of these. Well, I suppose that in this game I should never say definitely, but very much more than likely, you will only need one.

Boppy Pillow

Many parents expecting twins may not think to purchase a Boppy pillow (a firm, "U-shaped" pillow designed to assist moms with breastfeeding, babies with sitting up, or babies when they are playing) because they are often touted primarily as a breastfeeding support. Boppy pillows are invaluable for parents of twins. If you are breastfeeding, they provide value by holding the baby (or babies) at breast height without your having to hold the baby there yourself. (While now, holding seven pounds in one arm sounds like holding a feather, when my boys weighed that much, I can assure you they did not *feel* like a feather after a twenty-minute feeding!) For simultaneous bottle-feedings, when the babies are small, they can lie next to each other inside the pillow while you hold a bottle in each baby's mouth. If you are only feeding one baby at a time, wrap the pillow around your waist as you would if you were breastfeeding; having that support to rest your arm on will keep that arm from burning like mad from the accumulation of lactic acid. As the babies get larger, the pillows can help them to sit up, and they are also wonderful for supporting the babies as they lie on their stomachs, which helps them gain neck strength (under constant adult supervision). My husband wanted our babies' heads to be "on" as soon as possible, so he was a huge fan of strengthening their necks by putting them on their tummies, supported by the Boppy pillows.

Bottle Prop

You are probably going to need one of these. I don't think that any of us in the sorority started out with one, but nearly all of us ended up with one. It's critical. Why? Because at some point, both of those babies will need to eat at the same time and any strategies you had previously developed to accommodate them both simultaneously will no longer work—either because the babies are bigger, or squirmier, or decide that at that moment, they don't want to be next to one another.

There are various models to choose from; most are advertised in twin or multiples' magazines or on Internet sites that sell products for multiples. The model that many of us purchased was called The Bottle Bundle, from Little Wonders (www.littlewonders.com). It's almost like a mini Boppy pillow, so it's soft to the touch. It's shaped like a "U" with an elasticized band on top to hold the bottle, and you place it on your child's chest and around his shoulders in the manner necessary to keep that formula or breast milk flowing. Now, most of us quickly realized that the prop does not work fabulously on very young babies. Also, you often need to prop it further by placing a receiving blanket or burp cloth under it to lift the bottle higher so that the baby is getting more than air after three swallows. Many of us found success using the prop with the baby in his swing (in the reclined position) because it allowed the prop to be the most upright. The bouncy seat often made it more difficult because the baby was actually too reclined (or could bounce!).

Diapers

You can simply *never* have enough diapers. Just get a stockpile in a variety of sizes before the babies are born and you won't have to worry about running out in the middle of the night during those first few months.

The only real question to ask yourself up-front is: Cloth or disposable? I do not yet know of a woman with twins who has used cloth diapers, but if you really want to approach it this way, there are some diaper services that will come and pick up your old diapers and deliver fresh ones once a week or so. I remember when my father-in-law, who is a brilliant environmental engineer, asked me if I had ever considered using cloth diapers. I told him that I would be happy to consider it, if he would consider hopping a plane and coming over every time a kid needed a new diaper. I'm pretty sure that's where the conversation ended.

Another debate that is likely to ensue sooner rather than later is which brand of diapers to buy. It seems to be a commonly held belief that the Pampers brand works better for girls, while Huggies works better for boys. I have certainly found this to be true, but know of other moms who think the differentiation is ridiculous. Then, there are the generic diapers, which a lot of people really like. Others say that a paper diaper would be more absorbent. You will have to test-drive the choices and see what works best for you. If you end up choosing one brand and have a whole closet filled with another, just take the unwanted (and hopefully unopened) ones back to the store. More than likely they will be happy to exchange them for you.

Diaper Bag

Most "typical" diaper bags on the market are not the best option for a mother of twins. They are simply not meant to accommodate two of everything. You will need a bag that can be carried hands-free and one that will not bang against your hip and/or awkwardly hang from (and then fall off of) your shoulder as you push your Cadillac-size stroller. The sorority's recommendation is to purchase a well-outfitted backpack, one likely meant for outdoor excursions where you need the lightest, smallest bag possible that will accommodate water bottles, keys, and possibly a day's worth of other necessities. Look for one with a mesh water bottle holder on each side. I could easily fit two bottles in each side. Mine also had a mesh holder on the back where I often stored the formula measuring container, another set of bottles, or burp cloths (things you will need in a hurry and won't have time to rifle through a bag to find). If the diaper bag has multiple interior compartments, you can store diapers, wipes, a changing pad, some toys, and even extra clothes in case of accidents in one, then smaller items such as your keys in the other. When your babies get a bit older (say, around one year), a smaller, more "typical" diaper bag will more than likely work fine, should you choose to get one or have one that you received as a gift. At that point, you won't be as concerned about needing to take half of your home with you just to go down the street for a thirty-minute play date.

Be sure not to throw out the cute little complimentary diaper bags you will probably receive from your obstetrician and/or the hospital. No, they are not big enough to hold all of the gear required for an outing with young twins, but they do often contain valuable coupons or samples. Barb filled one with two water-filled bottles, two single-serving formula packets, diapers, wipes, and two changes of clothing, and stored it in her car in case of an emergency. That way, if—heaven forbid—she got into an accident or was heavily delayed by traffic, she didn't have to worry about further delaying a starving or wet baby.

Powdered Formula Travel Container

If you will be feeding your babies formula at all, I highly recommend the purchase of two formula measuring containers. These containers are often overlooked because they are called "Powdered Milk Containers" and their purpose is therefore somewhat unclear. These containers, often sold near the bottles, are small and divided into three or four compartments, each meant to hold one feeding's worth of powdered formula. If you are going to be away from home during a feeding, you can fill the pre-measured slots with the amount of powdered formula you will need for each feeding. If your babies are on two different formulas (which I recommend avoiding at all costs—it's just too confusing), you can measure out different formulas into each container, and mark them accordingly.

Clothing

The bottom line is that you will never feel that you truly have enough clothing for twins. The babies' closet will look like it is overflowing, and your husband will say that you positively, unconditionally do not need another item of clothing for the babies, and then suddenly, you will go into that closet to get two outfits and it will be empty. Why? Because you have not had time to do laundry in a week or notice that the contents of the closet have been slowly dwindling. I am not proposing that you buy until you drop. Over time, you will get into a pattern of doing laundry more often and that alone will solve at least ninety-two percent of the problem.

In the beginning, be sure you have plenty of gowns, pajamas, and onesies. You will go through them like you will go through caffeinated beverages. From spit-up, to diaper leaks, to your accidentally pouring half of your glass of water down your child's front because you've fallen asleep holding the water you were hoping to drink as they finished their bottle, you're going to need a lot of the basics in the beginning to keep you from *having* to do three loads of laundry a day. While I've become very cost-conscious over the past year, I can honestly say that in the end, the added expense of a few extra basic pieces is worth it to help save your sanity during the first few months. More quickly than you would believe, you'll learn how to bargain shop with the best of them to cover the next seventeen years of their lives.

MAMA'S GEAR

Headset Phone

This is a very important staple. You will want to have conversations with other adults (possibly even telemarketers) just to keep in touch with the outside world. It's hard to do that while juggling one baby, let alone two. Investing in a headset for your current phone, or a headset phone altogether if your current phone will not accommodate a headset attachment, would be invaluable. You will be able to do whatever you would be doing, plus talk at the same time! My sister got me a headset phone as a birthday/Christmas gift the first December after the boys were born, and it was truly one of the best gifts I have ever received.

Subscription to *Real Simple* Magazine

Until recently, I received so many magazines and catalogs in the mail that my husband wondered how bored I truly am during the day to have the time and the desire to subscribe to all of them. Since having the boys, I have cancelled subscriptions to all magazines except two: *Martha Stewart Living* and *Real Simple*. I think I still get *Martha Stewart Living* not because I have the time to make and can my own jelly or concoct my own apricot facial scrub from the apricots I grow in my Midwestern backyard (just kidding), but because I still harbor the hope that one day, I will have the time to do that should I desire. It's a fantasy thing. *Real Simple*, however, is a different entity altogether, and I would like to take a brief moment to extend my greatest thanks to its editors and everyone else who keeps it on store shelves month after month. This is the grandest magazine ever invented for the busy person. It's not terribly long, so you can actually get through it in less than twenty sittings. It has all kinds of short articles on making your life simpler and staying organized, two skills mothers of twins really need for staying sensible. The ideas are all realistic, low-cost, and low time commitment. I look forward each month to the arrival of this magazine, and I have used dozens of its suggestions to make life around this zoo more organized, less chaotic, and all-around more enjoyable.

Cute, Comfy Pajamas

Do yourself a favor and invest in a few of these prior to giving birth. You will be wearing them a lot, and you should enjoy them and feel cute and comfy in them. When you've been wearing one pair for four days, you won't want to take them off to wash them if you don't have another pair handy, so have at least one other pair around that you can throw on while the first pair sits in the dirty laundry—until your husband gets so desperate that he actually *does* the laundry. (And then pray that he knows to separate whites from the new, never-before-washed deep reds.)

Crockpot

Oh, what a miracle it would have been to realize prior to the boys turning eleven months old how fantastic the crockpot is. Did you know that you can make more than stew in a crockpot? You can make paella, pecan-rubbed pork, even stuffed peppers! My husband got me a fabulous crockpot recipe book for Christmas last year, and my mom brought one with her on a recent visit as well. I am now so loyal to my crockpot, it has it's own special resting spot in the pantry. I use it at least three times a week; I simply throw the ingredients in while the boys are napping in the morning and six to eight hours later, dinner is served! The meals are as varied as they are delicious. If you do not have a crockpot—get one. And splurge on a recipe book or two to go along with it; I've recommended two in Appendix B.

Sense of Humor

I've said it before and I'll say it again (and probably yet again before you reach the end of this book): A sense of humor is of *paramount* importance to successfully completing the first year. If there is a moment during which you simply can find nothing to laugh about, one will undoubtedly present itself to you just to keep the universe in balance.

Case in point: Our twins were about six months old, and I was having a long (and relatively heated) discussion with Barb, whose girls were born nine days after Jack and Henry, about the fact that husbands often don't seem to realize what a change their wives' lives go through when they have a baby (or two). Men continue to go off to work each day while the women oftentimes give up jobs, some friends, food, clean clothes, and occasionally, sanity. I felt as though I didn't know how to communicate to David how I was feeling without going off the deep end (little sleep and/or food can make one a bit cranky). That afternoon, the newsletter from our local multiples chapter arrived. Within the newsletter was a witty, clever summarization of most of the women of the world's feelings toward their spouses on any given day. Following is an excerpt, author unknown.

CLASSES FOR MEN AT OUR ADULT LEARNING CENTER

Sign up by June 16

NOTE: Due to the complexity and difficulty level of their contents, each course will accept a maximum of eight participants. Topics to be discussed:

- How to fill up the ice-cube trays, step-by-step, with slide presentation.

- The toilet paper roll—do they grow on the holders? Round-table discussion.

- Is it possible to urinate using the technique of lifting the seat and avoiding the floor/walls and nearby bathtub? Group practice.

- Fundamental differences between the laundry hamper and the floor. Pictures and explanatory graphics.

- The after-dinner dishes and silverware—do they levitate and fly into the kitchen sink? Examples on video.

- Learning how to find things, starting with looking in the right place instead of turning the house upside-down while screaming. Open forum.

> • Health watch—bringing her flowers is not harmful to your health. Graphics and audio tape.
>
> • Learning to live—basic differences between mother and wife. Online class.

After I stopped laughing, I questioned for a few moments whether this was a joke or not because frankly, such a class could be quite valuable. I gave the piece to my husband that night and said, "Honey, in a nutshell, this is what I'm thinking many days. However, when I think it, it's not quite so funny." It was perfect. I think he got it (as much as was possible) and the next evening, he arrived home from work with flowers in one hand and toilet paper in the other.

If you find yourself terribly upset one day that you are still in your PJs at 4:00PM, your hair is in a disheveled ponytail on top of your head, the house is a wreck, the laundry is piled to kingdom come, and it feels like it will be days before your husband gets home, just take a deep breath and really look around you. Try to get perspective on the fact that it truly could be worse. Then, just laugh—at the way you look, at the way the house looks, and at the fact that you are crying about it. In no time at all, it will be better. In no time at all, life will fall back into place. I promise.

All in all, this is the basic lowdown on gear. You will undoubtedly come up with several items that you find necessary—almost required—in the coming months that may not be on this list. Just know that the above will get you completely prepared to start the adventure in comfort and style.

THREE

0-3 Months:

Ready . . . Set . . . Feed!

TOP TEN MOST FREQUENT THOUGHTS DURING THIS PHASE

10. Are you sure I should wait only six weeks to have sex? Don't you mean six months?
9. I didn't know my body was capable of creating breasts this big.
8. Will these children ever stop eating—could they possibly be having *another* growth spurt?
7. Will they ever sleep at the same time—even for just fifteen minutes?
6. I cannot believe both of these babies were inside me at the same time!
5. While not exactly a fashion statement, a bag of frozen peas in my bra sure sounds good right about now.
4. How did I ever survive the days when we would not even go out until 10:00PM?

3. What ever prompted me to *want* to stay up all night?
2. Why is it that immediately upon diapering this kid, he decides he's got to go . . . again?
1. There are people out there juggling quadruplets, quintuplets, even sextuplets and septuplets at this very minute. (This one usually gave me all the perspective I needed to make it through a particularly challenging hour.)

THE ADVENTURE BEGINS

L et me begin by saying how impressed I am that you've found time to pick up a piece of reading material longer than a take-out menu now that your new bundles of joy are here! I think the first time I read something other than the now-infamous local pizza delivery menu was when the boys were about four months old and I was tearing through *The Baby Whisperer* yet again in an attempt to make Tracy Hogg's approach work for twins. I figure that either your twins have not yet been born and you're trying to get a head start (good idea!) or you have a supreme routine going that allows you to read at least a page a day. Possibly, your twins are five and you're just now finding time to read again and wondering how good your own creative solutions were! No matter how you got here, I'm very glad you're here.

WILL WE BE ALIVE AT THE THREE-MONTH MARK?

I promise the answer is yes, you will. The first three months are, in my opinion (and that of my girlfriends), the most challenging. More than anything, this is because you are trying to recover physically from the pregnancy and birth while adapting to the needs and personalities of your new babies. To be perfectly honest, each phase (0-3 months, 3-6 months, and 6-12 months) is not necessarily any easier or harder than another, just different. Actually, that's not completely true. It *will* get easier. My mom summed it up well by saying, "It's not a different ballgame, just a different inning." And that's a good thing because the longer you play the same game, the more skilled you get, the more shortcuts you develop, and the better you play.

What makes it all work during this phase? Many things. Mostly the repetition of several key phrases. Do whatever it takes to keep these thoughts running through your head. Post them above the changing table (if you have one), on the front of your feeding logs, on the front of the refrigerator, and/or on your bathroom mirror (which I realize you might be unlikely to look into that often!).

Mantras For Keeping Your Sanity

- I will sleep again.

- I will keep my sense of humor.

- I will be flexible.

- Nothing magical happens at the six-week mark. (Don't let this comment discourage you. The knowledge that the six-week milestone isn't as magical as you might have been led to believe will help in the end. One day you will wake up, a hurdle will have been crossed, and another will await. At least you will no longer be bored with the first one. When the babies were about four months old, I found myself saying with great frequency, "Crawl in different directions, crawl up the walls for all I care, JUST SLEEP!)

- It matters not if I shower each day or get into real clothes. After all, I've been dreaming of a day I could spend in PJs from dawn until . . . well . . . the next dawn.

- God would not have given us these babies if He didn't know that we could do it.

I've entitled this chapter, "0-3 Months: Ready . . . Set . . . Feed!" because that is really what this time is all about. You would simply not believe how much of the next three months are going to be focused, directly or indirectly, on eating. First, there's the babies' need to eat (a lot and often). Then, there's your need to eat. Then, there's the amount of analysis you will do around how much (and how often) your babies are eating and how that relates to the fact that they aren't sleeping. You'll analyze and analyze again, modify feeding schedules, find all kinds of ways to eat food yourself while juggling one or two babies, learn how many good foods there are that can be eaten with one hand, and then probably go back to another analysis of your babies' eating patterns, their sleeping patterns related to their eating patterns, and their eating patterns related to gas, constipation, and other common newborn challenges. Like I said, this phase revolves a lot around the concept of eating.

Know that these three months are going to be a lot of fun and a lot of work. Be good to yourself and focus on the "lot of fun" part. If approached the right way, this time will provide you with much laughter, many opportunities for bonding with your spouse, a newly acquired regard for the pleasures of sleeping for more than an hour at a time, eating a full meal while it's still warm, showering more often than once every three days, finding time to put on real clothes before the sun goes down each day, and a *huge* regard for clothes unstained by spit-up! It will also provide you with unmatchable blessings such as the newly formed bonds with your children, the feeling of a heart ready to explode when you see that first smile, the memory of a first "conversation," love for the smell of a freshly bathed baby, and joy of seeing your husband developing the most amazing relationships with each baby, just to name a few.

FEED!

As I'm sure you are aware, there are two ways to feed those beautiful babies of yours: breast or bottle. This is definitely a personal decision for each woman or each couple. Know that whatever decision you make is the right one for you, and be comfortable with it and confident in it. Do the best you can with whatever decision you make; that is all you can ask of yourself. Nearly everyone will have an opinion on whether you should breast or bottle-feed. The only people who will respect your decision to do either or both are other mothers of multiples. So, go with your gut and know that this sorority supports you 100 percent, no matter your decision.

BREASTFEEDING: WILL MY BREASTS EVER RETURN TO A NORMAL SIZE?

Much to the dismay of your husband, I'm sure, the answer is Yes. Not only will they return to a normal size, they will seemingly regress to the size they were just after you hit puberty.

Breastfeeding provides physical and psychological benefits to both mother and baby. Studies have shown that breastfeeding is an effective preventive mechanism for many childhood illnesses including ear infections, upper and lower respiratory infections, Sudden Infant Death Syndrome (SIDS), and allergies to name a few. Reduced rates of breast and ovarian cancer have also been shown among women who have breastfed.

When asked how they lost the weight of pregnancy so quickly, many new moms may respond, "Breastfeeding!" Breastfeeding causes your uterus to contract more frequently and your body to burn excess calories. Now, I breastfed my daughter and remember thinking at the end of the first three months, These calories appear to be going from my breasts right back onto my rear end (but I am usually the exception on a lot of things).

I remember the night my husband and I were sitting in our second of five Marvelous Multiples birthing classes at our local hospital and the lactation consultant came in to talk to us about breastfeeding. Everyone in the class was fixated on this woman. I think some were genuinely intent on breastfeeding their babies and others were truly interested in how this woman was going to explain with a straight face how breastfeeding two at once is done.

Each of us was given two baby dolls. This was the first time most of us had a true sense of what it would be like to have two babies at the same time. After all, we had all held the baby of a friend or relative—or in my case—my daughter, but two at a time was an entirely different proposition. Imagine my new friends Paul and Holly a few seats away who would be juggling three! The consultant began demonstrating some techniques for breastfeeding two babies simultaneously and it was then that the reality of what this was going to entail began to set in. A lot of folks remained determined and I heard some giggles as well as some comments such as, "OK, this isn't *too* bad," going around the room.

Honestly, it wasn't the "how" of breastfeeding two babies at once that had people's jaws on the floor, it was the "how often" of it. I will never forget the look on my friend Mollie's face as the lactation consultant began explaining just how often we could expect our children to eat each day. Eight to twelve times per day. Per baby. That's right folks, you've done your math correctly, and I could just see Mollie doing the math with her eyes. That could equate to twenty-four feedings per day. Now, how many hours are in the day again? Oh yes, twenty-four. And each feeding can take, say, thirty minutes including diaper change (or two) if feeding babies individually. So, I figured that left about one minute per hour to use the bathroom, eat, get dressed, shower, do dishes, make formula, tend to my two year old, and whatever other miscellaneous chores needed to be done. I'm fairly sure I just started laughing at that point, but I swear, I thought Mollie was going to cry.

It was in that moment that I made the conscious decision to do the best I could with the breastfeeding thing, but not to put any pressure on myself. After all, taking care of the babies could only be best accomplished if I reserved *some* semblance of care for myself, so I wasn't going to kill myself trying to breastfeed both babies.

Several of my friends used a breast pump as much as possible while supplementing with formula for as long as they could; several others went with formula from the get-go. Mollie (the "Oh my God, how many times a day did you say they were going to eat?" gal), who is now one of my closest friends, so cute you could scream, and has always been my grounding point as far as what's acceptable versus what's not acceptable, swore up and down before having her twin boys that she'd breastfeed . . . period . . . because it was the "healthiest" thing to do for the babies. Well, they wheeled that breast pump into her room five hours after her delivery, she took one look at it and commented to the lactation consultant that it was the most unnatural thing she had ever seen, asked the consultant to please get it out of there, and requested that a few cases of formula be delivered to the room as soon as possible. So, even with the best of intentions, plans change, and that's OK.

There are a multitude of positions you can use to breastfeed your babies simultaneously. I tried one of them once in the hospital. One baby decided he was finished long before the other, there was no one around, I was behind this whopping-big curtain, and I wanted to scream, "Um . . . could I get a little help here?" Had a nurse not come to check on me, I would still have one baby on my left breast and the other cradled in my right arm today.

Strategies for Breastfeeding Two Babies Simultaneously

When the babies are newborns, and both they and you are learning to breastfeed, it may be beneficial to have someone else help to position the second baby.

- Use the football hold. Place a pillow on either side of each of your hips. Put each baby on a pillow, on his side, with his feet pointing toward your back (holding the baby as you would a football as you run down the field). Cradle the babies' heads in your hands. Use extra pillows if necessary to support the babies' heads at breast level.

- Place one baby in the football hold and the other in the cradle hold. The cradle hold is the most traditional breastfeeding position. The baby is cradled across your front, on a pillow for support, with his stomach and chest touching your body (if the baby's stomach is pointing toward the ceiling, you're not positioned properly). The baby's head is cradled in the crook of your arm (his ear, not the back of his head, should be resting on your arm). Place the second baby in the football hold in your opposing arm. The head of the baby in the football hold will gently rest against the abdomen of the baby in the cradle hold.

- Place both babies in the cradle hold (baby's chest against your chest), with their bodies crossing each other's.

My boys were in the NICU for sixteen days after their birth. While they were there, I pumped as often as I could so they could get as many of the benefits of breast milk as possible; the hospital supplemented with formula as necessary. I believed that the colostrum they received in my early breast milk was important for them because they were premature, and I focused as best I could on drinking enough each day (beyond what I was sweating out due to the severe hormone drop) to accommodate my determination to give them at least a little bit of breast milk at each feeding. Additionally, the lactation consultant explained to me that by some miracle, a woman's body knows at what gestational age her babies were born and produces colostrum and then breast milk with specific properties to support the babies' unique needs. Knowing I could provide something specifically tailored to Jack's and Henry's physical needs that no other person and no formula manufacturer could provide gave me even more determination to do the best I could with that antiquated-looking breast pump—a "breast milk producing machine," really.

Once our boys came home, I tried as hard as I could to breastfeed each baby two or so times a day and pump when possible. Honestly, for me, it simply wasn't doable. By the fourth week, I was completely exhausted and could not take another look at that breast pump. Finding time to pump amidst everything else I was trying to do was the straw that broke this very tired camel's back. So, a formula-feeder I became.

Should you be determined to breastfeed in whole or in part, go for it! I do know of a woman who breast-fed her twins exclusively for the first year. It was a full-time job, but she was successful. There are many resources out there to assist you. Please take advantage of them as often as necessary.

Breastfeeding Resources

La Leche League International
An international resource for women committed to breastfeeding their children.
(847) 519-7730
www.lalecheleague.org

Nursing Mothers Advisory Council
This group is a non-profit, volunteer organization that serves specific counties in Pennsylvania. It is staffed by a group of women who have breastfed their children and are anxious to help others have a positive nursing experience. If you live outside of Pennsylvania, you can utilize the site's Help section or send an e-mail to the group to request further assistance.
(215) 572-8044
www.nursingmoms.net

Local Support
If you are not sure, check to see if the hospital where you delivered your babies has lactation specialists on staff. If you worked with one while you were there, do not hesitate to call her for assistance. They are always willing to help.

BOTTLE-FEEDING

Chances are, with more than one baby in the house, there will be some bottle-feeding going on—even if it's with breast milk—so that you can get some assistance from your husband or another helper. Chances are also high that at some point early on, your spouse will be at work and both babies will need to eat at the same time. There are two schools of thought on whether to bottle-feed babies together or separately. One is that it's far easier if your babies eat at different times because then you only have to deal with feeding one at a time. Obviously, the downside of this is that you're almost always feeding someone. The other way of thinking is that it's easiest if they eat simultaneously because that way, you only have to do one feeding every few hours, leaving you more time to eat, shower, or most importantly, sleep! The downside here, if you have to note one, is that feeding two babies at once requires a bit of coordination. You should certainly decide for yourself which method is easier and abide by it whenever possible. (Sometimes, no matter how hard you try to schedule it, both babies will need to eat at the same time, so better to be prepared logistically in advance.)

Obviously, a major benefit of bottle-feeding, whether with formula or with pumped breast milk is that on occasion (say, 3:00AM), you can get some assistance with the feedings from your husband. When I had my daughter, I breastfed. So, when she woke in the middle of the night, I was the only one on-call. With the boys, David could feed the one who was awake, allowing me to sleep until the next feeding, or he could help with the second baby, which was great since feeding two babies at once when you can't keep your eyes open is often an interesting challenge (but don't fear, there are solutions to this as well).

Strategies For Bottle-Feeding Two Babies Simultaneously

- Put both babies in their respective car seats next to each other, and hold a bottle in each baby's mouth. (There's no need to buckle them in when they are small unless you're going to pick up the car seat and move it somewhere.) In the beginning, you will want to burp them halfway through their bottles at a minimum or you will more than likely be wearing the contents of the entire bottle within fifteen minutes. When one baby needs to burp, there are again several methods from which to choose. One option is to stop feeding both babies, burp one, burp the other, and start again. If neither baby is patient enough to wait for his sibling's burping marathon, an option is to stop feeding both babies momentarily, take one baby out of his seat, lay him across your thigh, and pat his back while you resume feeding the other baby. Then switch.

- While the babies are still small, put them in one Boppy pillow and hold bottles in both mouths at the same time. Same strategy on burping applies here as when you're feeding them in their car seats.

- Use two couch or other pillows. Put one baby on each pillow and sit with your legs in a V-shape. Pull the babies in as close to you as possible, and hold a bottle in each baby's mouth.

- Use two bed pillows. Put one on your lap with the baby's head on the right side and the body facing left. Then, put the second baby on your right side, with his head next to your right knee and his feet underneath your right arm. Hold a bottle in each baby's mouth. My girlfriend Sonya swears by this one.

- Invest in a bottle prop. As mentioned previously, this can be very helpful if you need to feed both babies at once, especially when they get big enough (and wiggly enough) that it's difficult to feed them simultaneously by yourself. The prop isn't meant to substitute for your presence, just to help you out. REMEMBER NEVER TO LEAVE A BABY UNATTENDED WHEN USING A BOTTLE PROP AS HE COULD CHOKE. I had a horrible time getting mine to work in the beginning, but when the boys got a bit older, they did much better with it. So, if it doesn't work initially, do not dispose of it. Just keep trying! I know several women who have had success using the prop with their baby in a swing or car seat since each of these keeps the baby in just the right reclined position for feeding. I almost always had to fold up a small towel and put it under the prop so that the bottle was more tipped up. Otherwise, the bottle was always dropping and the baby could not get anything out of it.

- Feed the babies back and forth from the same bottle. This suggestion will probably elicit a big "whammo" from the medical community, but the bottom line is that this book is a guide from moms who have *been* there to moms who are *going* there and honestly, so many moms of twins do this—some in the closet, some publicly—but they're doing it nonetheless. Barb used to put Olivia and Kambria in their car seats, fill a bottle to six ounces or so, give one baby an ounce, then the other, and back and forth until they had each finished. This meant fewer bottles to wash as well as fewer instances where you would make a whole bottle, the baby would eat nothing, and you would find yourself pouring the contents down the drain. When Barb admitted to all of us that she was doing this, it started the debate over whether to share bottles between babies

> during the same feeding for fear of spreading germs or whatnot. Within a week of this discussion, we were all allowing our babies to share bottles—not necessarily by giving one baby an ounce then the other an ounce, and so on, but by feeding one baby who was screaming and only took an ounce and then giving the second baby the remainder of the first baby's bottle. Personally, I decided that Henry's sucking on Jack's cheek while drool was running down it was probably spreading as many germs as his feeding from the same bottle. If the babies were clearly sick, I did not allow them to share a bottle. It ensured that I could continue to consider myself a responsible parent.

A final benefit of bottle-feeding, and one that I didn't figure out until the boys were about four months old, is that you can (and should) make your formula in one big batch—whether the babies are on the same or different formulas. This is more for your mental health than anything else. There will be days when you truly don't think you can mix another bottle, and the ability just to pour it from its container will save you hundreds of dollars in therapy. Once mixed, the formula is good for forty-eight hours in the refrigerator, so as soon as you get a grip on how many ounces you'll go through in forty-eight hours, you could actually find yourself mixing formula every other *day* as opposed to every other *hour*. In addition, many formulas, when mixed on the spot and shaken vigorously, develop a lot of bubbles that can make a baby's tummy uncomfortable. When you pre-make your formula, those bubbles dissolve as it sits in the refrigerator; once you give your babies their bottles, the formula is bubble-free.

There are many ways to mix the formula. Here are the ones that have worked for us:

Strategies for Mixing Formula

- Get a big Tupperware container, fill it with water to the desired ounce line, add the appropriate amount of powdered formula, and shake vigorously. If your babies are on two different formulas, get two different containers and label them with the "owner's" name.

- Get one of the marketed "formula-mixing" containers. They have a paddle attachment in them that helps dissolve the formula and avoid lumps. My girlfriend Holly is a big fan of this product.

- Blend it! One day, Mollie was sick and tired of shaking and stirring and still having lumps in her formula. She called me and said, "I've had it. I'm blending!" I had never thought of doing it that way, but I can now tell you that I instantly became a proud every-other-day blender of formula. I also bought this incredible container by SlimLine (I found it at Target). It is only about four inches wide, but as deep as your refrigerator, and it has a spout on it. So, you fill it with formula (it would actually hold about four days' worth of formula, though while I've taken a lot of shortcuts, I know that's one I can't mess with), and it takes up the tiniest space in the fridge. When you need to fill a bottle, you just put it underneath the spout and pour! It's ingenious. It's not easy to clean, but since I only had to do it every other day, I managed.

Some people mix their formula at night or first thing in the morning (though I highly recommend doing it at night because even though you'll be exhausted, if you're lucky, it will be quiet for a short period of time). They then pour bottles for the next day based on how much their babies are offered at each feeding. Mollie's babies were always offered between four and eight ounces, depending on their age, so this worked for her. My boys, however, took varying amounts based on when they last ate, what kind of a mood they were in, and possibly, what day of the week it was, so I just poured each bottle as needed (and was usually still wrong on the amount one way or the other, but . . .).

One issue that several of us came up against to which we couldn't find an answer to save our lives was whether we could give breast milk and formula or actually breastfeed and give formula in the same feeding. There seemed to be a recurring concern that mixing breast milk and formula was causing the babies to have difficulty digesting the concoction. It appeared that if you did one full feeding of either breast milk or formula and then the next of the other, it was OK. However, if you tried to combine breast milk and formula into one feeding— either by putting both into a bottle or by breastfeeding first and then, upon discovering that it didn't seem that your baby got enough (or was screaming so loudly that you convinced yourself he still *had* to be hungry) supplementing with a bottle of formula—the babies had difficulty digesting the meal. In the end, the recurrent conclusion of many in the sorority was that you could not combine breast milk and formula into one bottle, and if you breastfed first, you had to will your body to produce enough milk to satisfy the baby for that feeding so that you didn't have to supplement! I will note that there is no medical reason not to mix formula with breast milk. It is done frequently (and successfully) in the NICU (and it was even done with my boys in the NICU; they tolerated it well at that time). Furthermore, many women are able to combine breast milk and formula over the course of the entire first year without it adversely affecting their infants. I just know that many of our babies seemed fussier after a feeding during which breast milk and formula were combined. Check with your physician if this issue arises for you, but know that if you begin to believe that the combination of breast milk and formula in one feeding is possibly causing an issue, you are not the first to draw such a conclusion.

According to Dr. Kristine Liberty, a pediatrician in Naperville, Illinois (and my personal hero on many days), some newborns simply digest breast milk more easily. The proteins and/or lactose in some formulas may cause certain infants to experience an increase in gas due to the immaturity of their digestive systems. Often, it might not be that the combination of formula and breast milk is the culprit, but rather the brand of formula. In this case, a formula change would likely be sufficient to solve the problem. Dr. Liberty recommends that parents discuss the brand of formula they plan to use with their pediatrician because every infant is different. Additionally, the discomfort a baby appears to be experiencing after a feeding may not be a gas-related problem. "A condition known as gastroesophageal reflux affects many infants and may be causing some discomfort," notes Dr. Liberty. Don't try to self-diagnose your child when it comes to apparent discomfort related to feedings. Let your pediatrician help you work through these issues, which many times miraculously fix themselves as the babies grow and their digestive systems mature.

NIGHTTIME FEEDINGS

One of the challenges that we all really worked on (for obvious reasons) was our nighttime strategy. My husband used to get me crazy because every night at about 10:00, he would begin a conversation that went something like this:

David:	OK, Liz, how should we handle the feedings tonight?
Liz:	What do you mean?
David:	Well, do you want to do the midnight and the 4:00, and I'll do the 2:00 and the 6:00?
Liz:	So, you somehow know that not only are they going to wake together for all feedings, but also that they are going to do it at 12, 2, 4, and 6?
David:	Well, no, but just to get a general idea of the schedule . . .
Liz:	David, if I had any general idea of the schedule, don't you think I'd *have* a schedule by now?
David:	OK, so how are we going to do it?

This conversation went around and around (and around) until suddenly, a baby was crying and then we were debating who was going to get up. (Of course, David was convinced it should be me since I was apparently penciled in for the midnight feeding. However, I quickly reminded him that we had never successfully *completed* that discussion.) Then, miraculously, the other baby would wake up, the debate was over in a hurry, and we were both dragging ourselves to the nursery.

Figuring out your nighttime strategy will be very helpful. You can go into the evening hours with some idea of what to expect and plan your evenings accordingly.

Logistics for Nighttime Feedings

- Designate which of you is responsible for any feeding before 11:00PM, and which is responsible from 11:00PM-4:00AM; then, whoever was on-call until 11:00PM goes back on-call at 4:00AM. This allows someone to sleep from, say, 8:00PM-11:00PM (which I could never do, but Mollie did it very well), someone to sleep from 11:00PM-4:00AM, and then someone to sleep from 4:00AM until whenever he or she has to get up for work or has to get up because the *other* is off to work and a baby is crying.

- Alternate feedings. Usually, during this phase the babies will either wake together to eat or one will wake while the other is eating. Therefore, you can opt to take the first feeding, your husband the second, and on and on. We tried this, and the only challenge was that oftentimes a feeding could go on seemingly for hours since one diaper change turned into three or a baby who had only taken two ounces would suddenly decide he needed more. It is a strategy though, so give it a shot if you think it might work for you.

- Play "Baby Roulette," also known as "Pick-A-Baby." This option requires that you and your husband each claim a baby. Whenever "your" baby wakes, you're in charge of that feeding and diaper change. Realize that you'll probably have a baby who is a bit better at sleeping than the other, and if you're anything like me, you'll pick the "wrong" baby the first night, and switch to the "good" baby the second night, only to discover that they have reversed their roles, and not for the last time! This is definitely a time to have a sense of humor, but I realize it can be tricky at 3:00 in the morning.

- Take the hungry baby downstairs each time he or she needs to eat. Barb and her husband, Tim, did this (which is probably why Barb is in far better physical shape than I am at this point). Tim is a very light sleeper, and so in order for him to get his time in dreamland, Barb would feed the girls downstairs in the family room. This worked for her because she could keep the bottles in the refrigerator, heat them in the kitchen, and watch some very interesting infomercials while she fed Olivia and/or Kambria.

I truly believe that our best strategy was the one whereby we designated "hours of responsibility." Yes, you will squabble when your shift ends in three minutes and a baby suddenly begins to scream. (Do what I did: When you're dealing with less than three minutes until the next shift starts, try to fake that you're completely zonked until the clock hits that magic number and then politely tap your husband on the shoulder and say, "Honey, I'm so sorry, but you're on.") This strategy got my husband and me the most consecutive hours of sleep. Four hours of sleep a night is not sufficient, true, but four consecutive hours is far better than thirty minutes here and thirty minutes there totaling four hours, believe me! Even with this strategy in place, we tried as best we could to be flexible. There were nights when one of us was on-call, and the other was painfully aware that our spouse was struggling (babies were screaming so loudly I was sure the police would show up any minute). When this happened, the one of us who was technically off-duty usually marched in and did what he could to assist the other—change a diaper, finish feeding a bottle, whatever—and then marched back to bed.

Nighttime Feeding Entertainment

- Talk. Regarding the issue I mentioned earlier of not being able to keep your eyes open while doing middle-of-the-night feedings, one solution is to attempt to use this time to have a half-coherent conversation with your husband, should he be up with you. You could discuss your daily budget, overall long-term financial plan, dream vacation, the fact that you need a bigger home, or the days when you could sleep for twelve hours straight.

- Sleep. You won't believe how easy it will be to nod off during a feeding—and how easy it is to wake up almost instinctively just as your baby finishes his bottle.

- Eat. Keep some snacks by the designated feeding area. You will more than likely be feeding a baby only to hear that oh-so-beautiful sound of your stomach growling. It will be then that you will think to yourself, "Gosh, I haven't eaten in a *long* time!" As you continue to focus on this fact in the dark, quiet night, you will get more and more hungry. Again, a psychological thing (as so much of this is). So, keep some snacks nearby.

ORGANIZATION: THE KEY TO SUCCESS

And is it ever! If you weren't organized before, I guarantee you will be now. If you *were* organized before, you're going to "kick it up a notch," as Emeril Lagasse would say.

I went into the hospital suddenly at thirty-two weeks in pre-term labor, and came home for only twenty-four hours before I went into unstoppable labor and delivered at thirty-five weeks. What the boys' little vacation in the NICU gave us that was extremely positive was the chance to get things as ready as time permitted. But to be perfectly honest, the best way to organize is just to live it and see what works for you. It won't be more than about fifteen hours before you'll have some high-priority challenges that need solutions. Fast. And you'll come up with them just as quickly as we all did, believe me. Remember, God would not have given you multiples if He were not completely and utterly confident that you were up to the challenge. There are some strategies that each and every one of us needed and employed, however, so I will pass them along with the hope of saving you at least a few steps.

First, a feeding/diaper-changing log is essential. There are many ways to do this. Most of us created a binder or clipboard with pages that had columns labeled "Time," "Ounces," and "Diaper." Each baby had his or her own colored pen, which was tied with string onto the rings of the binder. We'd make an entry for the time the baby started eating, how many ounces she ate, and whether she had a wet or dirty diaper.

Barb had what I think was an excellent strategy in that she had two clipboards, one for each baby. One was printed on blue paper and one on white, so the pen color didn't even matter. The only potential mishap would be losing one of the clipboards, but the bottom line is that as long as you don't lose a baby (well, for more than a minute or two), you're doing great.

Once the babies get older and are eating less frequently, you can get a wipe-on/wipe-off board and affix it to your refrigerator. We continued to mark feedings on this until the babies were almost eight months old, not so much because we were concerned with the amount of intake in those later months, but because we needed to know when each kid had eaten. You'd be amazed how even at six months, a baby can cry and you think, "I fed one of you thirty minutes ago, but which one of you was it?" Of course, it was usually at this same moment that I realized I hadn't changed my two-year-old's diaper in about ten hours either. It can get you crazy, so just be organized about it. Like they say, sometimes all you can do is laugh or cry and, well, I've preached this one before.

Another challenge that will require an immediate solution is the preparation of bottles for nighttime feedings. After all, each baby could potentially eat up to four times between 10:00PM and 6:00AM. That's a total of eight bottles. There are multiple strategies to choose from here:

Nighttime Formula-Feeding Strategies

- Get a wire basket with handles (the kind you used in college to take to the showers), and stock it with eight bottles filled with the number of ounces of water you think each baby will eat per feeding. Also, take a can of formula or a pre-measured formula container upstairs. This way, when a baby needs to eat, you just make the formula on the spot. It's at room temperature, so there's no need to warm it.

- Put a refrigerator in your room. I sincerely wish we had done this, and to be honest, if I could go back and do it again, this is one thing I *would* do differently. I'd put the refrigerator in when I was pregnant so that in the middle of the night when I woke up starving, I could grab a pudding, a glass of milk, or a large turkey sub. You can pre-fill your bottles and store them in the refrigerator, and then use a bottle-warmer to heat them up when a baby is hungry. Now, my girlfriend Sonya's husband, Bob, swears that not only should you have a refrigerator in your room, but a microwave as well, to heat the bottles. Sonya felt this was getting a bit excessive and the whole topic of warming bottles in the microwave is one we'll get to later, but it is an option, if you've got a big bedroom and a crazy husband (no offense, Bob).

- Do not forget to make use of the hospital in terms of those cute little two-ounce ready-to-feed formula bottles. We got a stash of these as we left the NICU, and on many nights when my husband or I was so tired we couldn't make out the ounce line on a bottle with even the best squinting efforts, they saved us. When the babies are young, they may only take in one or two ounces at a feeding anyway, so these bottles are the perfect size. When they don't finish them—and worse, when they barely take one sip—you want to just die as you pour the leftovers down the drain, but . . .

- Several people I know did purchase the ready-to-feed formula just to use at night. The only problems with this are that the formula—once opened—has to be stored in the refrigerator. So, you're stuck having to get a refrigerator for your room and then heat the bottles, or make trips up and down to the refrigerator several times a night. Also, the ready-to-feed version is quite a bit thicker than the powder. Barb likens the ready-to-feed formula to Slim Fast shakes. Some babies don't seem to tolerate the consistency well, so just be aware of that.

Whether using breast milk or formula, there are several methods for heating bottles. In the beginning, everyone wants the safest way to do it. So, start with that (this would be Option One or Option Two listed below). A third (and more controversial) option follows:

Heating Bottles

- Fill a big cup with very warm water. Heating a bottle this way takes several minutes, but Mollie used to start heating the bottle when she knew a baby would be getting hungry, and then would change the baby's diaper before his feeding while the bottle was warming up. When his diaper was changed, the bottle was ready. If the bottle gets too warm this way, dunk it in some cold water for a minute or two.

- Use a commercial bottle warmer. These can be purchased at stores like Target or Babies "R" Us. I used one with my daughter, Grace, but found that it always Over—or under heated the formula. Barb had great success with the Avent Express Bottle Warmer and never found that it Over—or under heated her bottles.

- Use the microwave. (I want to pull the neck of my shirt up over my head as I say this.) Once your babies are a bit older (around three months of age, probably), you'll begin looking for even more shortcuts, if for no other reason, variety. One of the options I bet you will be wondering about—and hedging on—is using the microwave to warm bottles, especially since by this time, I know you'll be making your formula in batches and either pouring bottles outright every morning or pouring them on demand. Either way, your formula will be cold and unless your babies could not care less (and there are some who couldn't) you'll need to warm the bottles—and fast. Yes, I know, using the microwave to warm formula is a very big no-no according to all the books and healthcare professionals. I understand where they are coming from. However, what drives me nuts is that I believe that any book written by a mother of twins who advises against it is only doing so out of fear of being criticized by a pediatrician somewhere. (And yes, I am a little bit afraid of being criticized by my own the next time I don their doorstep.) Mollie was the last of us to adopt this method of heating bottles. As I've mentioned, she does follow those books to the letter. However, when her boys were nearly seven months old, she and her husband took them out of town for the weekend. In desperation she had to warm their bottles in the microwave. She never looked back.

> NOTE: DO NOT HEAT BREAST MILK IN THE MICROWAVE. Heating breast milk by microwave has been shown to destroy some of its protective properties. The best way to warm breast milk is by partially submerging the bottle in a large cup of very warm water.
>
> A good rule of thumb is five seconds (on high) for every ounce. This is dependent on your particular microwave, of course. Be sure to invert (not shake) the bottle multiple times once it's been warmed to ensure even distribution of the hot spots. A baby's mouth is much more sensitive to heat and cold than an adult's and will burn easily. Also, warm the bottle in the microwave with the nipple off. This allows the heat to escape the bottle. If you are nervous about using the microwave for *any* reason, use another method. The sorority does not want any part of this first year to be any more uncomfortable than it already might be!

THE DOORBELL THAT JUST KEEPS RINGING

About as certain as it is that your babies will be eating more frequently than the clock ticks is the fact that your doorbell will be ringing almost as frequently (and hopefully not *more* frequently!). Everybody wants to help during this time. The problem is, not everyone's definition of help will match your own. We had a lot of people who thought they were helping by popping in to take care of the babies while I cooked or cleaned. What I really needed was someone to do the more unpleasant (and hard-on-the-body) tasks of cooking, cleaning, laundry, or grocery shopping while I fed, changed, fed again, changed again, and with any luck, snuck in a fifteen-minute nap.

Traffic Control

- Place a sign on your front door asking visitors to *knock*, rather than ring the doorbell. Inevitably, you will have just gotten a baby to sleep after hours and hours of rocking, singing, or doing creative jumping jacks (without actually jumping, of course—beware the stitches!) only to have someone ring the doorbell. Also inevitable is that this same person who is oblivious enough to ring the bell will also be oblivious enough to ring it two or three times in a row—just in case you didn't hear it the first time (or to signal their extreme excitement about arriving).

- If the visitors are people who will be coming over frequently—grandparents, aunts, uncles—ask them if they would mind bringing a package of diapers or a dinner with them when they come. At this stage, it's all sort of a trade—you bring sustenance or other necessities, you're welcome to visit with our babies.

- Be sure to let visitors know what *you* need. Don't feel obligated to give in to their needs. Let them know if what you really need is someone to come and do laundry or the dishes or prepare a meal since you haven't eaten in two days. Try to make it clear up-front that these visits early on aren't so much to take care of the babies as they are to take care of you, which enables *you* to take care of the babies.

- Make sure everyone washes their hands before handling the babies.

- If you've managed to create even the smallest semblance of a schedule (or even if you just want to *think* you

75

have for your mental health), do NOT feel that you should deviate from it to accommodate visitors. If the babies are napping when visitors arrive and don't wake up until after they leave, apologize and mention that you hope they can come back soon when the babies are awake. If visitors call ahead of time, let them know when you *think* the babies *might* be awake, but remember that in the early weeks, although visitors will undoubtedly want to see the babies, what *you* really need is help.

- If your idea of help at any point is just to turn those babies over to a trusted friend or family member, by all means do that. Even someone sitting with them while you take a nap might feel like the greatest vacation you've had in years.

BATHING

This activity has simply never been one of my favorites. I know a lot of people love bathtime, and find it an incredible opportunity for bonding while letting the babies play in the water. I have personally never felt that way. It's always been an in . . . clean . . . out activity. Even when I had my daughter, bathing was not one of my favorite things, and I only had one baby to contend with. However, because I had only one child to bathe, it was something I could do fairly regularly and quickly if need be. With the boys, that just wasn't the case. First, there were two of them (obviously). Second, I had a toddler running around whom I could not leave alone while I bathed the boys. Third, making two trips up and down the stairs to get the boys to the bathroom left me with little energy to do the actual bathing. And last, bending over—not once, but twice—the little bathtub that was on the floor or in the tub left me in need of a chiropractor (but, of course, with no time to see one).

There are some easy ways to make bath time more pleasant. First and foremost, always wait until your babies' umbilical cords have fallen off and, if applicable, your son's circumcision has healed before you bathe them submerged in water. Until those two things have occurred, just give sponge baths as needed, especially around their bottoms and necks (where formula has undoubtedly found a home and turned into cottage cheese).

My greatest advice for bathing two babies, especially if you have other children—but even if you don't—is to use the downstairs bathroom sink or kitchen sink. Until the boys were about three months old, I bathed them one at a time in the powder room sink because it was smaller and I felt as though I had more control over their little bodies. Once they turned three months old, I moved to the kitchen sink. Using the sinks as bathtubs proved indispensable for several reasons. First, the height was perfect. No more bending over and bothering an already sore lower back. I could have everything I needed right at arm's length. The space was compact so the boys felt secure, and my toddler was always within earshot if not eyesight. One thing to be aware of is whether you have a draft coming through your kitchen or bathroom. In that case, start by turning off all ceiling fans and closing all windows while doing the baths. My boys were literally in, washed, and out in about ninety seconds, so the opportunity for getting chilled was extremely low.

Additional Strategies for Bathing Young Babies

For starters, always have all your supplies at arm's length before you begin bathing. Have your baby shampoo (I highly recommend a body wash that cleans both their hair and their body with one product), towel, washcloth, cotton balls, and so forth, all there ready to be put to use. It has been said a million times, but just so I know I've put it out there, NEVER LEAVE YOUR BABY UNATTENDED IN THE TUB OR SINK FOR EVEN A SECOND. Babies have drowned in as little as an inch of water.

If you are not as vertically challenged as I am, try putting a baby bathtub inside your own bathtub and bathe them that way. It's good to find a baby bathtub with a little drain in it because you can drain the soapy water out and then refill with clean water without having to lift a heavy, water-filled tub. Also, you can put a baby bath sponge inside the tub. These sponges, which are very inexpensive, fit the length of the tub and keep babies from slipping around. They are also wonderful to use when you are doing those initial sponge baths. Just put them on your floor or counter (never leave the baby unattended while you are doing this) and they have a soft cushion to lie on as they get their sponge bath.

Depending on the size of the baby, it may work (especially toward the end of this three-month period) to bring the baby into the bathtub with you, clean him, and then hand him out to your husband, who will dry him, clothe him, and proceed to hand you the next baby. This is a time-consuming way to do baths, but it can be a fun, bonding experience—*if* you are in a bonding mood or looking for something fun to do on a Friday night. (I know, every night is Friday night, or Monday night, or Wednesday night . . .)

My friend Mollie used to put a small basin she "borrowed" from the hospital on her kitchen table. This gave her a small tub at waist level. Her husband would hold one of the babies in the water and she'd do the washing. Then, they would bathe the second baby. She also used cotton balls to apply baby oil when the bath was finished to make their skin soft. That is, until she discovered the miracle of baby oil gel, a product that provides the same benefit and far less sliminess than baby oil.

UNSOLICITED ADVICE: STORIES FROM THE TRENCHES

This is a topic for which I have great passion. I could truly write an entire book on the comments you are likely to receive, the questions you are likely to be asked, and ways—polite or otherwise—to respond (depending on your hormone level that day, how tired you are of the particular question, and how nice a person you are to begin with).

One of the hardest places from which to receive unsolicited

advice is your own family or that of your husband. In most cases, these folks are merely trying to help, but frequently, the reality is that their comments can leave you feeling inadequate, unprepared, and possibly angry. The best way to deal with this, in my opinion, is to be as calm as possible. The last thing you need at this time is a big hoopla over something that in the end, no one has control over but you. People can comment until the cows come home about how you should be doing this or should not be doing that, but when the day is done, they will go home (hopefully) and you will do things the way you see fit.

I know many people who's family was nothing but helpful after their babies were born. They were there to cook, clean, wash clothes, shop, whatever was needed. Some were even available in the middle of the night! Unfortunately, not everyone is lucky enough to have this experience. If you are one of those people, don't worry, we're going to get you through it.

One of my friends found success by saying enthusiastically, "Thanks, we've got it covered" (as she bit her bottom lip and silently repeated to herself "I passed the test on whether I could manage twins when I proved I could handle you—most of the time"). If the offenders just won't back off, perhaps it's time to curtail visits (and have your husband answer the phone) either until they get it (which isn't likely), until Dr. Phil is available for a personal house call to help them "get real" about what they are doing (again, not likely), or until you are better rested, more confident in your parenting, and otherwise better able to deal with them.

Questions and comments from perfect strangers are a whole different ballgame. You simply would not believe how interested perfect strangers can be in the conception and management of your babies. I could not believe how many people asked if my twins were conceived using fertility drugs. After all, no one ever asked if my daughter was conceived using fertility drugs! Now, if I had been pregnant with nine babies, chances are, fertility measures were used (though I do believe there was a woman in China who recently gave birth to natural sextuplets). Twins are so common nowadays not only because of the increased use of fertility, but because women are choosing to wait until later in life to conceive, which increases the potential for them to drop more than one egg per cycle. It shocks me that so many people still believe that you have to be on fertility to conceive two babies at once.

Here are some of the more common questions you are sure to be asked along with our humble opinions on the reasons for these questions. So that you are not left totally hanging, I've also provided a variety of responses that you can have at the ready. One issue that's interesting to work through is when to bite your tongue and when to just let it rip. This also applies, of course, to meddling by family members.

"What kind of fertility were you on?"

Never, *never*, will I understand how people feel comfortable asking others—especially perfect strangers—this question. I've decided that it's all in the name of insane curiosity about how others live their lives. Perhaps these people are just having a really boring day, are unnaturally curious about the personal lives of others, or are poorly affected by the way the stars and moon aligned the previous night. Never have I had someone ask me about my fertility experiences who was actually going through fertility and wanted to "share." Those folks are usually just as reserved as I am on the topic, if not more so. All that being analyzed and pointed out, the time comes just to move on and attempt to find a comfortable response. Some people in the world are likely open and honest about the way in which they got pregnant. They want to share it with the world. (I don't know any of these people, but they probably exist somewhere.) If you are one of these people and some stranger on the street seems oh-so-interested in the "how" of your pregnancy, then by all means be open and tell them.

One of my favorite responses is to just say, "Oh, are you having trouble getting pregnant?" People are usually not nearly as comfortable answering this question as they were asking their initial one, so this often ends the whole discussion in a hurry.

Another option is to respond, while wearing the biggest smile you can muster, "Why do you want to know?" You would be positively amazed by how many questioners have no *clue* why they want to know and will simply move on.

A final favorite response of mine is to smile and simply say "Wow, that's a really personal question!" (and then just keep walking). It's kind of like saying, "None of your bleeping business!" with the nice tone that a mother of twins should use.

"Which side of your family do twins run on?"

This is usually a harmless question, and while you will start to be royally irritated by it, I find that most people who ask it are genuinely just trying to make polite conversation. They are not the same people who will ask what form of fertility drugs you took or in what fancy position you and your husband had to "do it" to conceive more than one baby at the same time. When people ask about twins running on one side or the other of our family, I usually just comment that they run on neither side. Few people understand that twins can only "run" on the mother's side. Only the mother can pass the tendency to naturally release more than one egg to her daughter. Though I'm sure they would love to claim otherwise, a man's sperm simply is not strong or appealing enough to force a woman's ovary to release yet another egg. Of course, identical twins have nothing to do with genetics. An egg splitting is purely a random act.

"Wow, I'm sure glad it's you and not me!"

Hate this one! It's just so unnecessary and as my mother always says, "If you have nothing nice to say, don't say anything at all." Some people just feel like they *have* to say something—I have no idea why—so they say something relatively stupid. Do not waste a moment on these folks. Here are two options: Put on your best half-smile and keep walking or comment as nicely (or as cynically) as you would like, "Me, too!"

"How do you do it?"

OK—another one of my not-so-favorites. But here's what I've come to dissect from this comment. When people ask, "How do you do it?" they don't really want an answer. This is just translation for "*I* could not do it." And no, clearly they could not or they would have twins with them as well. Nevertheless, I realize that— albeit completely subconsciously—they are paying me a compliment. They are saying, "I could not do it. You *are* doing it. You are an amazing human being who I only wish I had the fortitude to be able to call my friend," and, therefore, I've taken to accepting this statement simply as a poorly worded compliment. I usually respond (so I'm not totally rude to these kind, complimentary folks) with: "Oh, they make it easy." If, however, you are having a particularly bad day, provide the inquirer with the answer to his or her question. Go on and on, beginning with "Well, I get up around 6:30AM. I go down and get breakfast ready for the troops, and then I fly like Mary Poppins back up the steps and sneak silently into their room to pick out their coordinating outfits for the day. I subsequently slide down the banister, and skip into the family room to ensure that all the videos, books, and other learning toys are lined up and ready to go . . . " By this point, the questioner is trying to get away from *you*.

There was the day, however, when nothing had gone right and I was sure bedtime would never arrive. A woman with whom I was sharing an elevator sighed and said, as though just thinking about my day made her as tired as I already felt, "*How on earth do you do it?*" I looked at the woman, at the boys, and back at the woman only to say, "You know what? I don't have any idea!"

"You sure do have your hands full."

Again, a real original comment and one you're likely to receive at least seven times each week, depending on how frequently you get out. It's really just a not-so-clever combination of "How do you do it?" and "I'm glad it's you and not me." Again, folks who utter this are simply not comfortable with awkward silences. Just smile and let your mood on each particular day determine how broadly or faintly you deliver said smile.

The braver women of the world (or perhaps those who are just in a really sour state) conjure up more brazen responses to some of these comments and questions. One example, uttered by a woman who was in our multiples class with whom we have unfortunately lost contact, still makes me chuckle. She was grocery shopping with her husband one afternoon when she was about six months pregnant with her twins. The woman behind her in line overheard her talking about the babies. This woman actually followed her out of the store, hailed her down, and asked if she had been on fertility. To this, the pregnant woman responded, "Excuse me. Did I ask you if you douche?" I about fell out of my chair when I heard this. It's definitely the extreme way of saying, "That's a really personal question and none of your business," but after all the inappropriate questions we've each received, my girlfriends and I have gained more and more respect for that woman's guts to deliver that particular response.

I actually had a woman approach my sons and me as we walked to their physical therapy appointment at the hospital and comment on how cute they were, and how *big* they were (my husband is 6' 6"). She asked how early they were born, how much they weighed at birth, you know—all the stuff that people are so fascinated with for reasons unbeknownst to mothers of multiples. She asked if they were breastfed and I said, "No." She looked at me and said, rather condescendingly, "They're NOT?" I said, "No, they're not." She said—nose up, eyes down—as if she were providing me with as-yet-unknown, valuable information that could change the course of history, "Well, you *can* breastfeed two, you know." I should have said, "Oh, how old are your twins?" but I'm simply never ready for these people at the moment they strike, so I just said, "Well, *technically*, you can, yes" and made a beeline for the therapy room.

My friend Holly, who has triplet girls, has of course received numerous comments about funding college *and* three weddings, but the strangest comment she ever got was from a woman who said, actually to Holly's husband, Paul, "Wow. Imagine how much you guys are going to be spending on tampons in twelve years!" That one left them both speechless and if you knew Holly, you would understand what a feat that is.

The strangest comment I have ever received was from a man who asked nothing about whether my boys were identical (which they clearly are not), their names, or my use of fertility drugs, but inquired as to how many minutes apart they were at birth. I was so struck by this—no one had ever asked me anything like this—that I actually had to say, "Excuse me?" I then told him they were twenty-eight minutes apart, and he wanted to know who was first. I told him, and that was the end of that. Still intrigues me to this day.

Barb and her husband, Tim, have been asked on numerous occasions if their girls are twins and Tim is dying to say, "No, this one is two weeks older."

My boys look so different from one another that I am constantly asked if they are both mine and when I answer "Yes," inevitably, the person asks how many months apart they are. I want to say, "You realize that they would have to be at least nine months apart for that question to get a genuine answer. Do they look nine months apart?" Different? Yes. Nine months different? Nope!

Along those same lines, Mollie was in the mall one day and a woman came up to her and asked if her boys were twins (although fraternal twins, they are each other's clone, so this question was semi-ridiculous to begin with). Mollie said, "Yes," and the woman said she assumed that Tommy was the older one because he was bigger. Mollie commented that actually Kevin was older. The woman said, "Oh—by how many weeks?" Again, where do you even go with that?

"Which one is smarter?"

I'm still speechless over that one; though I've only been asked it once!

So, the lesson is, be prepared for unsolicited questions and advice left and right until, I'm sure, your kids reach the age of eighteen. I'm already prepared for, Are they in the same class?—along with the questioner's unsolicited opinion on whether that's good or bad—Do they have different friends? and on and on. I'll probably always be unprepared in the moment, but at least in hindsight, I hope to have some good responses to share with my friends.

GETTING THOSE BABIES ON A SCHEDULE

Undoubtedly, you have been told one too many times that the key to regaining your sanity (and your beauty) is getting your babies on a schedule. This is true, to some degree, but putting too much pressure on yourself too early to accomplish this feat may quickly push your sanity in the wrong direction. Remember, two-week-old babies do not have the ability to go seven hours without eating. They do not have the ability to operate off of a perfectly constructed schedule. And if, by chance, you have miracle babies who have the ability to be on a schedule from Day 1, I can almost guarantee that they are not operating on each *other's* exact schedule. At least, not yet. They will one day, for sure, and certainly before they are anywhere close to one year old. Be patient. The key here is not to expect too much too soon. Do the best you can and everything will work out just fine.

Your main goal during this 0- to 3-month period as far as your babies' schedule goes is simply to try to get them on a feeding schedule.

Don't worry about nap schedules at this time. Don't worry about nighttimes until the end of this period when you could start introducing a "typical" bedtime depending on your babies' habits and personalities (it might be 8:00PM; it might be 10:00PM).

Newborn infants do not have an innate feeding schedule. Notes Dr. Liberty, "It is not uncommon for a newborn to feed every one and one-half hours. If the mother is breastfeeding, it may seem to her that she is nursing all the time. It is not uncommon for a breastfed infant to nurse for thirty minutes (obviously with twins, that is a thirty-minute feeding times two!), so the interval between feedings may be quite brief. As infants gain weight and mature, they become more efficient with feedings and will be able to tolerate longer stretches between those feedings. I recommend that parents watch for cues from their infants that signal hunger, such as rooting. If the infant nurses or takes the bottle vigorously and seems content afterward, then he was hungry. Many times infants just need a source of non-nutritive sucking, and a pacifier may be a better choice. Eight to twelve feedings in a twenty-four-hour period is recommended for the newborn."

Honestly, if you can get your babies onto a reliable feeding schedule before they hit three months of age, you should write your own book on how to do that alone. So often, twins are born prematurely and simply take longer to reach a point where they can reliably take a consistent amount at consistent intervals. During these early months, it will also often difficult for you, as the mother, to feel comfortable proclaiming with confidence that the baby who has been screaming for two hours and seemingly eating for three is *definitely* not hungry.

The best approach is to try to establish set feeding times for your babies. Try to get them to eat every three hours or every four hours, whichever seems to work best in your situation. Realize that the babies will go through several growth spurts during these three months. (You will question whether they are going through a growth spurt during this time as frequently as you will question whether they are teething in later months, believe me.) Those spurts will require that they feed more frequently for a few days. By the time you have nearly given up on establishing a feeding schedule, and are sure you have tried everything, the babies will hit that three-month mark. It truly becomes easier (the feeding part, at least) once this occurs.

We'll go into greater detail in the 3-6 Month section on how to effectively get these babies operating simultaneously on all schedule-related fronts, feedings included.

WHERE DID ALL THESE DISHES COME FROM?

The only time when you will have more dirty dishes than you have when your babies are drinking formula every three to four hours is when they start eating solid food. But don't worry, we have a couple of chapters before we get there. My hands, and those of most of my girlfriends, were nearly destroyed before we had our "aha" moments and did the following. Start these practices from the beginning and your hands will only age by a year or two in the next twelve months as opposed to ten years in two weeks.

Maintaining Age-Appropriate Hands

- Ensure that you have enough bottles and nipples to last you twenty-four hours without having to wash them. This is very much worth the extra money (though it's not that much extra, really). Wash all bottles/nipples in the dishwasher nightly, even if there are only three nipples and two bottles. You will feel so much better not to have to unload a stuffed dishwasher each morning, and you will start each day with a clean supply of bottles.

- Be sure to invest in a pair of rubber gloves for washing dishes that cannot wait until that nightly dishwasher run. Otherwise, within about three weeks, your hands will be so chapped you'll want to die. For a holiday gift-exchange

---

> our first December after having our babies, the sorority members all exchanged lotion!
>
> - Have a bottle of nice lotion by your kitchen sink that you can apply after each handwashing. Some of the thicker lotions like Eucerin, Cook's Lotion by Crabtree & Evelyn, or No-Crack® Day-Use Super Hand Crème (I get mine at Restoration Hardware) have been some of my favorites.

FROM EMPTY CLOSET TO OVERFLOWING LAUNDRY BASKET

My most important piece of advice for this challenge is: Beyond doing what's necessary to get it to hang on the hanger, do not button anything before putting it away unless your name is Holly. One night, a few of us went over to her house to watch her triplets so that she and her husband could get out for a couple of hours. She brought down their "nighttime onesies" (these were exactly the same as the daytime onesies, only "clean"). The girls' pajamas were completely buttoned and even, I believe, ironed. (By the way, we also learned that evening that Holly had created bar graphs to depict the girls' eating patterns over the first couple of months. Each girl was represented by a different-colored line on the graph. Holly was using this graph to ensure that none of them was developing eating habits severely opposed to the others. So, that about says it. She's a personality type that I don't even believe has been identified yet, but that's the kind of person God gives triplets to because otherwise, I truly believe at least one of them would disappear under the sofa for a month or so.)

Additional Laundry Solutions

- Put dirty clothes directly in the laundry room so that you don't have to stare at them spilling over the edge of the laundry basket in the babies' room, and run laundry when you have a free minute; if it doesn't make you too nervous, designate the running of the laundry to your husband. (Another thing I've found is that by and large, God doesn't give twins to mothers who have incapable husbands, so I feel confident that there are some daily tasks you'll be able to ask your husband to take charge of.)

- For stain removal, try Mother's Miracle, Clorox 2, and/or Biz. We have each had great success with all of these products in removing numerous stains.

- Save frequent sheet changes by putting sheet protectors in the cribs (the kind that go over the sheet). There are narrow ones that will become ineffective once the babies start moving around (I always worried that Jack would somehow get his head wedged between the sheet protector and the sheet), and there are larger ones that cover the whole crib sheet. Also, as mentioned in the Gear section, get a mattress protector that fits like a pillowcase over the mattress. This way, when you go to change the sheet, you don't pull off the mattress protector every time you pull off the sheet!

ALL THOSE DIAPERS!

The only thing more voluminous than the number of baby clothes you will accumulate over the first year is the number of diapers you will dispose of each day. There is a large need to have a receptacle at-the-ready for the all-important job of containing them until the trashman comes.

We recommend using the Playtex Diaper Genie, Baby Trend Diaper Champ, or some such product initially. Many people keep one upstairs and one downstairs. However, with more than one baby, know that that thing is going to fill up *fast!* Many people I know (except Mollie, but again, she's often the exception) found an alternative (and larger) disposal unit pretty quickly, such as a large, lidded trash can designated the "diaper can" in the garage.

While you are still changing diapers during the night, keep a Diaper Genie upstairs and a trash can inside your garage for your daytime changes. (When the diapers get bigger and you're changing less during the night, you'll probably get rid of the Genie and just put them all outside.)

COMMON EVERYDAY PROBLEMS

I asked Dr. Liberty to help with some questions that all of the sorority sisters had day-in and day-out related to common, more medically-based, newborn challenges. Here are some of her insights.

Gas

"Gas pain is a common problem in newborns. Many times, an infant will draw his or her legs up to the abdomen when gas pain is present. Parents may want to try gentle rocking or use an infant swing or vibrating chair to alleviate gas. Infant massage or laying the baby across your lap on his or her belly may also help. Over-the-counter infant gas relief drops may be helpful, however a phone call to your pediatrician first is advisable. It is possible that a formula change may be helpful as well, but parents should discuss this approach with their pediatrician before making the decision themselves. If gas is a frequent problem, I would encourage parents to discuss it with their doctor. Prolonged crying during which an infant appears inconsolable may be a sign of something more worrisome and parents should consult their physician."

Diaper Rash

"Many pediatricians recommend against the use of diaper creams in the newborn period. Frequently a diaper rash during the first four to six weeks of life will improve by using a gentle cleanser or plain water to clean the diaper area. Leaving the diaper area open to air for periods of time is often helpful as well. A yeast rash is common when infants/toddlers are in diapers. Usually the irritation/redness appears in the folds of skin in the diaper area and often around the scrotum on little boys. This type of rash does not always resolve with traditional over-the-counter diaper creams. Parents should talk to their physicians about an anti-yeast cream. Any blistering, bleeding, or persistent rash in the diaper area usually requires additional therapies. In this case, the infant's doctor may have the family use two or more creams simultaneously."

Constipation

"Intermittent constipation can occur in newborn infants. Breastfed infants may only have bowel movements every few days. Sometimes parents perceive this as constipation. If the stools are soft and passed easily, it is not constipation. Difficulty passing stools from birth may signal a more significant problem and an evaluation by a physician is recommended."

Spitting Up

"Newborns may spit up frequently due to gastroesophageal reflux. This condition results from a weakness in the muscle that separates the stomach from the esophagus. As a result, stomach contents pass more easily into the esophagus, often resulting in spitting up. Most infants outgrow this condition without any intervention (approximately fifty percent by six months and ninety percent by nine months). Frequent spitting up is of concern when the infant is not gaining weight or seems to be fussy/irritable between feedings. Projectile vomiting is also of concern and warrants an evaluation by the baby's physician."

Baby Acne

"Neonatal acne is a response to maternal androgens. It usually occurs between two and four weeks of age and may persist for the first four to six months. It consists of inflammatory (red) pinpoint marks on the skin, mixed with tiny pustules (pimples). Neonatal acne occurs mainly on the face and scalp. Treatment varies depending on the severity. Gentle cleansing of the skin is recommended, as abrasive cloths or harsh detergents will make the condition worse. Acne can be treated with mild anti-inflammatory creams."

Cradle Cap

"Cradle Cap (Seborrheic Dermatitis) occurs commonly in infants. It is due to an overproduction of sebum and results in a shiny appearance on the scalp with a collection of scales adherent to the scalp. The scales may appear white to yellow in color. Cradle Cap improves with frequent hair washing and gentle exfoliation using an infant hairbrush, soft toothbrush, and/or the pad of your finger. (It is OK to exfoliate over the soft spot.) For more severe cases, you can use a dandruff shampoo, but be careful to avoid the eye area. Baby oil may be rubbed into the scalp to help loosen the scale."

Dry Skin

"At birth, a full-term newborn's skin is usually soft and smooth. Within a few days the skin will start to appear dry and cracked, especially around the ankles and wrists, due to the shedding of the stratum corneum, which accumulates before the infant is born. During this process, topical lotions can be used to hydrate the skin."

ADDITIONAL SOLUTIONS TO EVERYDAY ISSUES

Use Your Friends' Pediatricians

Not literally, of course, unless you've got unbelievable health insurance and a lot of free time on your hands, but you can use these resources without actually visiting their offices. Within our sorority, we see between three and four pediatric groups, with one to three of us using the same group. When one or both of our babies has gotten sick or had another issue such as gas or cradle cap, it's been interesting to call each other and find out what advice each others' pediatricians have given for the same ailment. The pediatric group I go to is what I consider medically-focused. More often than not, they have a medicinal solution, rather than a holistic or natural one, for issues. Barb's pediatrician, on the other hand, is more holistically focused; she uses medicine, especially in the case of a raging infection that requires antibiotics, but for the less-problematic stuff, she likes to try something more natural first. So, when my son Jack had a horrible case of baby acne, my pediatrician recommended a 1% hydrocortisone cream. Barb's pediatrician recommended using a washcloth to gently dab the baby's face with diluted chamomile tea. This became a running joke, actually, because before long, it seemed that she was prescribing diluted chamomile tea for everything from baby acne to constipation, but it did just as good a job in some cases (though not the baby acne) as the medicinal solution I had gotten. The bottom line is that if you have a pediatrician you trust and you trust your girlfriends as well, none of the solutions is likely to be harmful (provided the pediatrician is actually degreed), and having some different things to try and different perspectives will only make you feel more in control. You can run alternative solutions by your own doctor if it makes you feel better. Barb's pediatrician has a carrot soup recipe that she swears by as a cold remedy. Barb does now, as well, since her girls were better within two days of ingesting it (at eight weeks of age) and my boys still had their colds a week later, taking four to six doses of PediaCare a day.

Siblings

Many twins are born to parents who have no other children. Yet just as often, it seems, twins are born to parents who have at least one other child. When Jack and Henry were born, Grace had just turned two. This was a good age and a bad age. It was good because she was really too young to understand what was happening to her life or feel too terribly displaced by the boys (though I understand this potentially has more to do with the fact that she's a girl). It was bad because she was two! She was still in diapers, still learning to define herself and assert her independence, and still very dependent on David and me for everything from playing with her and showing her how much we loved her to getting her dressed and cleaning up after her (though amazingly, she did learn how to work the TV, the remote, and the VCR by herself very quickly.).

I cannot tell you how many people asked me how much harder it was to parent newborn twins with a two year old. At the time, I was as amazed to report as they were to hear that it wasn't bad at all. I had no idea how blessed I was to have Grace at the age she was when the boys were born. I have since decided that two or younger and five or older are the best ages for an older sibling when multiples are introduced into the picture.

She truly ignored the boys for the first six months of their lives. Then, they turned six months old, she turned two and a half, and I was no longer commenting to anyone how easy it was to have a toddler as well as twins. She wanted to interact with the boys, but she did not understand why she couldn't tackle a six month old. She wanted to feed them, but did not understand why they couldn't eat her pretzels. It was at this point that I think she started to feel the blow of their presence in terms of the attention and time they took away from her.

The situation became difficult in a hurry. As much as I wanted to spend time with each of my children, there was a reality that had to be addressed: I had three children under the age of three and only twenty-four hours in a day. I did my best to spend quality time with Grace in the evenings—often taking her with me on shopping trips to the grocery or Target—or scheduled some time with her during the boys' rest time or before her bedtime to do a puzzle or play "Hide and Go Peek." But, there were days when, during the boys' rest time, I needed her to rest because *I* needed to rest.

Things were the most difficult around the time Grace turned

three. Happily, my husband showed up one evening with a new book for me entitled *Parenting Your Strong-Willed Child*, by Rex Forehand, Ph.D. and Nicholas Long, Ph.D. This gift beat any large-carat-weight diamond at that point. I read that book and did exactly as it recommended. I did the best I could. And that's all any of us can do. We acknowledge the situation for what it is and then we do what we are capable of doing to fix it. If you find yourself in a similar situation, use the resources you have available to you. If you can find time, read (or skim) some books on dealing with the dilemma. Perhaps invite a friend of your child's over for an hour or so to play every once in awhile. If you have relatives nearby, ask them to come over and play or see if you can take your older child there to play for awhile. The issue really is attention, and in the end, I doubt your child will mind where it comes from.

The most important thing to do for your older children during your pregnancy and especially after the birth of the babies is to continue to make them feel important and loved. I know what you're thinking—Duh! The most successful thing I did ahead of time was stock up on some coloring books, puzzles, and other inexpensive, small items that I could pull out in a hurry. If Grace was feeling left out, and I had to feed a baby (again), I could pull out a new little "gift" which got her so excited that she forgot all about how left out she felt.

It is also important to nurture the relationships between your older child and the babies, though know that this may be a slow-going process. How well and how quickly this relationship will begin to cement itself will depend on many factors—how old your older child is, how secure he or she feels, etc. Don't expect too much out of anyone too soon. While some people found it "sad" that Grace pretty much ignored Jack and Henry for the first six months of their lives, I was elated by it! I did not have to worry about her attempting to pick them up while I wasn't looking, playing horse with them on the floor, or playing hide and seek with them, choosing to hide a baby!

In the end, even after reading and following the program outlined in *Parenting Your Strong-Willed Child*, I learned that I could spend twenty-four hours a day playing with Grace and some days, it still was not enough. That realization was a blessing because it took some of the guilt away regarding whether or not I was paying enough attention to her and including her enough despite the strain placed on my time by having three children who were all so young. At the end of the day, your kids just need to know that you love them. They need to feel secure in your home and in your love for them. You do the best you can for all your children, and yourself, and then you go to bed!

Developing Relationships with Each Baby

At first, these babies are going to sleep a lot. Personally, I think they've got the right idea. I have never understood toddlers who throw a tantrum at the mere mention of a nap. I would *kill* to have someone tuck me into my bed every afternoon and say, "Honey, you just sleep as long as you would like."

With all the articles and books on the market that emphasize the importance of bonding and developing a relationship with your babies, I believe many women have come to believe that means you must begin this pattern of education from Day 1. Nothing could be further from the truth. The education, for lack of a better word, that you need to give your babies now is the knowledge that you will always be there for them; that when they cry, you will pick them up (well, provided you aren't juggling their sibling). You will feed them when they are hungry. Your voice will be the one that they hear primarily during the day and through the night. The bond you are creating with your babies simply by feeding them, rocking them, or singing to them is enough right now. It is all they need to feel secure and loved.

Do not feel too pressured by all the products on the market designed to stimulate the babies during this time period. Less is more right now for all of you. Not that Baby Mozart videos don't come in handy even in the early days when you need to scarf down a bowl of Cheerios, but you do not need to feel that you should read 3.7 books to each child per day or do the Baby Einstein flashcards at least once before lunchtime. There will be more than enough time (and products) for stimulation and playtime in the months ahead. And when that point arrives, you will often look back with fond memories at how quiet it was in the early days (and with no memory of how much you were feeding those babies!).

FOUR

3-6 Months:

The Schedules Begin

TOP TEN REALIZATIONS/
PONDERINGS DURING THIS PHASE

10. The "I need more time to heal" excuse isn't going to fend off your husband's desire to "have relations" indefinitely!

9. Is she teething? I think she's teething. Maybe not. No, I think she is. Well . . .

8. *When* will I be able to get back into my old clothes?

7. I have got to get out of this house!

6. *How* do I get out of this house with two babies?

5. With what money will I shop if and when I manage to get out of the house?

4. Are they ever going to sleep through the night twice in a row?

3. Four months is too long to go without a haircut.

2. Will I ever watch *Friends* again?

1. Uh oh, I think they are starting to think about crawling!

THE SCHEDULE EMERGES

The goal of this period—and the triumph that most parents of twins are unbelievably eager to achieve as soon as possible—is to get these babies on a schedule. For the record, it just so happens that about every three months, you will be mentally ready for some new challenge—any new challenge— as long as it's new.

Getting one baby on a schedule is not always the easiest accomplishment. Getting two or more on a schedule—and the same schedule—is interesting, but doable. The key here, obviously, is to get these babies on the *same schedule*. Otherwise, you might have Johnny on a great schedule, and Jimmy on a great schedule, but you are never going to sit down by yourself for more than six seconds.

The best way to go about this is to start by vowing you won't allow yourself to feel overwhelmed by the prospect of doing it. You are going to start slowly and move your way up. By the time your babies are eight or nine months old, they will practically work like clocks. Now, I realize what you are thinking: Eight or nine months old? I won't *make* it until then! But you will, and it will be here sooner than you think.

According to Dr. Liberty, infants develop better sleeping habits when their hunger cycles are regulated. "Parents can encourage a routine by offering feedings at regular intervals. They may also encourage more predictable sleeping habits by putting their infants down to sleep at regular times. Newborns may initially sleep for only twenty to sixty minutes at a time, however the length of their 'naps' will increase by the time they are four to six months old, as their sleep cycles mature."

The women with whom I went through this whole adventure (and with whom I am still muddling through it) and I agree wholeheartedly on at least one step of this scheduling thing: Step 1 is unconditionally to get the babies napping in their cribs. Not in swings, not in Pack 'n Plays in the middle of the family room with the TV blaring. Definitely not in your arms. Dr. Liberty concurs. "Parents should start their infants sleeping in their own crib/bassinet as soon as possible (especially before four months of age). Infants can get used to sleeping in car seats, swings, or their parents' arms and it may become a difficult pattern to break." If your babies are already napping just fine in their crib or cribs, give yourself a great big pat on the back and treat yourself to some chocolate ice cream tonight.

There are several trains of thought on how to get babies to nap simultaneously in cribs. At about the three-month mark, your babies may or may not still be sharing a crib. If they are, and one isn't disturbing the other by moving around too much, feel free to encourage them to nap together in that crib. Most of our babies were in separate cribs at this point. One issue a lot of us ran into was that one baby would fall asleep and then the other would start screaming and wake up baby number one again. As always, there are several solutions to this. One option is to separate the babies into their own rooms. Barb did this and it worked well. The babies still bonded beautifully despite spending their napping and evening hours apart, and Barb and Tim probably got about fifty-seven percent more sleep than the rest of us during that time period.

We weren't lucky enough to have an adequate amount of bedrooms to accommodate letting the boys have their own, so we explored a few other options. We contemplated putting one baby's crib in the boys' closet. (This isn't nearly as abusive as it sounds. Their closet is a walk-in, and I didn't even have a closet this size until . . . well . . . I still don't, but that's another discussion for another day.) Another option is to set up a Pack 'n Play in another room—say your bedroom—and let one baby nap in that and let the other baby nap in his crib. Try to ensure that the baby who naps in the Pack 'n Play always naps in the Pack 'n Play. It is important that each baby becomes familiar with the environment in which he or she is expected to nap—sort of follows the Pavlov theory.

I tried this approach, but neither of my boys was too keen on sleeping in our bedroom in the Pack 'n Play, for whatever reason. Finally, I just bit the bullet and decided that they would have to learn to sleep in the same room. And they did. I soon discovered that if one cried and woke the other, the one who woke up was on the verge of waking anyway. If he was truly in a deep sleep, he didn't wake up when the other cried.

One issue parents have a concern about—and one that a few in the group experienced—is that of separating the babies out of the crib they had been occupying together. Will they miss each other? Will they become anxious, wondering where their sibling is? Mine could not have cared less, but Mollie's boys were *none* to pleased when they were informed that it was time to get a bit independent. Mollie's and Gary's solution to this was simple: They put them in their own cribs, but pushed the cribs together so the boys could see each other and sense each other's presence. Each night, they would move the cribs apart by about two inches until the cribs were at their "final destinations." The separation was gradual and the boys handled it just fine.

One important note: If you are going to separate your babies into different rooms, please do it early on. You would be surprised how early the babies will become accustomed to each other's presence during sleeping hours, and will be devastated to be deprived of each other's company. Jack and Henry barely interacted during their first eight months of life, but from four months of age on, from the minute one was put into his respective crib, if the other didn't follow suit within ten seconds, the screaming became ... well ... deafening.

Along with being screamed at by the boys for separating them into their own cribs, Mollie discovered that they were not doing a happy dance about being asked to get onto a reliable schedule. She found success by following the principles outlined in *Healthy Sleep Habits, Happy Baby*, by Dr. Marc Weissbluth. By the way, I highly recommend this book. It is entirely devoted to the process of getting your babies to sleep well. There is an entire chapter devoted to handling colicky babies (and the sleep strategies are modified as your child gets older). It provides detailed instructions on how to manage your baby (babies, in this case) during those first few weeks versus during later months. Obviously, what you can and should expect in terms of scheduled sleeping will vary as your child grows; you would not force a baby to adhere to a strict napping schedule when he is only three days old. It discusses how long to let a baby cry, how flexible you can be with errands and other unscheduled activities, and addresses common sleep problems. In the sorority girls' opinions, Dr. Weissbluth's approach is reasonable; he never professes that you may simply never go anywhere between the hours of 9-10:30AM, 1:00-3:00PM, or 5:00-6:30PM again. I know several people who have successfully used his strategies with twins. Go get the book, feign a headache, sneak up to your bed, and start reading.

Truthfully, the worst part of all this "scheduled napping" is that if you have a two-story house, you really will tell your husband one evening as he walks in the door, "Honey, we're moving to a ranch." This is because you will feel like you are making about 1,000 trips per day up and down those stairs to take the babies to their napping zones. Try to bear with it. It's good exercise and it's going to be worth it in the end.

Work on the morning nap first. An easy rule of thumb is to put the babies down for their morning nap about two hours after they wake in the morning. If you are experiencing life as I did, you're thinking, Great, one baby gets up at 5:00AM and the other at 6:00AM so I'm already hosed! Have no fear; this issue is short-lived if it occurs at all. There will come a time when, unless one baby is significantly more tired than the other (and this will happen occasionally), they will get up at about the same time in the morning. Barb's girls—who, remember, have separate bedrooms—still get up at different times and they are now ten months old. However, because Kambria gets up around 7:30, if Olivia isn't up by 8:00, Barb wakes her up so that the girls have breakfast together and start the day on the same schedule. Olivia is none the worse for wear for having been awakened early. (And I know, you hate Barb already because her girls sleep so late. I'm right there with you, but secretly, she's still one of my best friends.)

Once you've got the morning nap going, work on the afternoon nap (or naps). A typical attempted schedule for our group was to feed both babies a bottle when they woke initially, if it was very early. Because my boys got up every morning between 5:00AM and 6:00AM, there was *no* way I was going to do a formal breakfast at that initial waking. But they would not go back to sleep without something. So, before my husband jumped into the shower, he would feed them both a bottle. They would then go back to sleep until 7:00 or 8:00. Some of my girlfriends' babies didn't wake up at all until 7:00 or later (and yes, I hated them, too, for awhile). They simply started the day with breakfast.

Typical Schedule to Attempt

Unreasonably early waking	Bottle
8:30ish	Breakfast
9:30ish-11:30ish	Morning nap
Noon	Bottle
1:30ish	Afternoon nap
5:00	Dinner
*8:00	Bedtime bottle
8:30	Bedtime
*11:00	Bedtime bottle

* Your babies may go to bed successfully at 8:30PM and sleep until 4:00AM or so. Or, you might find that they still need that 11:00PM bottle in order to be able to make it until 4:00 or later. Schedule this last bottle whenever you need to in order to make your evening as quiet as possible.

These times are complete estimates. When your babies are still young, they will most likely have an early evening nap plugged in to the schedule as well. Once they reach six to eight months, you'll get fairly good about knowing when they will need to eat and sleep as well as what you can get away with regarding morning errands. When they were nine months old, I learned that my boys could skip the morning nap if I needed to be out and about, and then they would go down earlier in the afternoon. One word of warning: DO NOT assume that because your babies skip the morning nap they will sleep for four hours in the afternoon! I would often put my boys down around 12:30PM and think, OK, I've got three hours on my hands. I'd start some major project, only to hear them whimpering two hours later. The good news: If they skip the morning nap and take only a short afternoon nap, you can push that bedtime up and do your project in the evening. For every downside, there is almost always an upside. Keep this perspective and you will have survived the first year before you know it.

BEDTIMES

One key point to remember through all this bedtime stuff is that technically, sleeping through the night only means sleeping six hours straight. I remember when the nurse at my pediatrician's office told me this with Grace. I looked at her like she had told me Christmas was going to be off for the next seven years. When I finally regrouped, I said, "So . . . you mean . . . if she falls asleep at 9:00PM and wakes up at 3:00AM, she has technically slept through the night?" She answered, "Yes." I think my exact response was "Well, that's crap!" I then wanted to get hold of the medical practitioner who came up with that timetable because it was undoubtedly a man—without children—and I feel he should have had his license revoked. I mean really, it would feel better to have the nurse say "OK, Mrs. Lyons, your child is not sleeping through the night yet," rather than cause me to question why I look like holy hell; after all, "She's sleeping through the night!"

Anyway, hopefully I've saved you the utter disgust you would have otherwise felt when informed of this rarely mentioned fact by your pediatrician. The truth is that even if your babies fall asleep at 9:00PM and wake at 3:00AM, it is oh-so-much easier than when they were waking every two hours on opposing schedules. You and your husband can switch nights or each feed a baby, thereby significantly cutting down your away-from-dreamland time. So, while you're not out of the

I'm-not-snoozing-through-the-night woods yet, you've made a definite step in that direction.

Another point on this once-a-night waking: Don't change the babies' diapers unless you can tell that they really need new ones. More often than not at this point, they can go ten hours or so without a diaper change. Avoiding it will get you back to bed more quickly and will not prompt your babies to wake any more than they already have. They can have the bottle they need and doze right back off. If they don't realize that they are awake to begin with, they won't know they are eating in the middle of the night and learn to rely on doing so.

At some point during this phase, you will determine an acceptable bedtime for your babies. It may be as early as 8:30PM or it may be as late as 11:00PM. The time will be determined by a variety of things, not the least of which are your babies' gestational age and weights at birth.

Once you establish their bedtime and are confident that they can go six hours or so without needing to eat, you should have a plan for dealing with those nights when one or both of the babies wakes up long before the six-hour mark. The sleep-teaching process really has two components: Getting the babies to be able to fall asleep on their own in their beds, and getting them to *stay* asleep until they are waking from true hunger.

If a baby (or two) wakes up and you think, "They cannot *possibly* be hungry," check on him or them to ensure that they aren't stuck in an uncomfortable position or in need of a diaper change. If all is well, quietly reassure them with your voice and *do not pick them up!* I cannot stress this enough. You are not being cruel here. If you feel that you must pick up that baby, be prepared for the fact that you will be doing it the next night, and the next, and the next because what the baby is learning is that—barring a true physical need—if he cries loud enough and long enough, you will do what he wants. It's amazing how quickly babies can train their parents!

If you'd like, you can follow the example of Jamie and Paul Buckman from *Mad About You*, sit outside the door, and be in "pain" with your child or children. Or, you can get earplugs. Or, you can turn up the volume on the TV so high that you are concerned it might combust right in front of you. You can go downstairs and vacuum. Try something, anything, to keep yourself from giving in. I remember one day I was telling Mollie that I felt so abusive for forcing the boys to cry in the middle of the night, and I was concerned they were learning they could not count on me. She snapped me back to reality as only Mollie can. She said, "Liz, if they had a real need, you would help them. You always do and that's how they know they can count on you. They need to learn to go to sleep and to put themselves back to sleep when they wake up prematurely. It is a life skill; they don't realize that yet, but you do. You are their mother and you know best. You are rational and logical and they are not. And, by the way, when you do give in, once you leave their room, they just lie back in their crib and whisper 'sucker!' "I about died of laughter, and I knew she was right. I worked really hard and within a week or two, we had two all-night sleepers (well, most nights). I finally had complete confidence that they *could* sleep through the night, so when they woke at midnight, I knew either that something was wrong or that they could go back to sleep if I gave them time. It was easier to convince myself on their "off nights" that I wasn't the most abusive mother on earth.

STARTING SOLIDS

I will address this topic in the 3-6 Month section even though, most likely, you will not start your baby on solids until he or she is closer to six months old. If your doctor has not advised you to start solids early for medical reasons, let *me* advise you—WAIT! I know, the thought of doing something new, especially if these are your first babies, is unbearably exciting. However, a week into it, you'll be wondering why on earth you decided to start this before you had to, and by then the babies will be too used to it to be able to back up. Let me elaborate. Today, if you have to go somewhere, you pack bottles. Once you start food, you will have to pack food, spoons, bibs, and possibly a feeding chair of some sort. You will also have to find an easy way to feed them this food in their strollers, car seats, or your lap. Today, when you feed them, you only have to clean their bottles (and potentially change their outfits if they spit up). Once you start food, you will have to clean the highchairs, the bibs, the floor, the babies' faces, and maybe even wash their hair since they will likely put their food-covered hands in it and try to do the old shampoo job themselves. It's a lot of extra work just for a little excitement and the knowledge that you are doing something new. So, if you are at a point where you feel like *must* have something new in the routine, incorporate a trip to the library once a week or something.

The other reason I mention solid foods in this chapter is so you can prepare yourself. Yes, there is preparation here, too. (Don't worry, by the time this first year is completed, you will be so skilled at being prepared, you will be prepared for being *unprepared!*) For starters, get a jump-start on ensuring that you have the proper equipment for feeding solids. As I mentioned in the section on gear (I believe that repetition is often highly appreciated by mothers of multiples), highchairs are good, but in my experience and that of my girlfriends, booster-like seats are better. Why? They don't take up nearly as much room as a highchair because you just strap the booster onto a kitchen chair. Also, they are easily transportable for those times when you will be at someone else's house during a mealtime. The booster seat made by The First Years has a three-position recline. You can fully recline it when your babies first start eating and may not yet be capable of sitting upright. As the babies gain more strength, you can make the chairs more erect.

Another decision to be made is whether you will buy commercially prepared baby food or make your own. Now, like breastfeeding versus bottle-feeding, this decision is entirely up to you. I have no issue whatsoever with commercially prepared baby food—except for the price and at times, the variety offered. Knowing what we spent per week for our daughter to eat the commercial food, we estimated that we would spend approximately $300 a month to feed the boys. Gives you real insight into how quickly 47-cent items can add up! In addition, there are so many of us with twins living within a two-mile radius of each other, we knew that we would have to strategically schedule our baby-food trips to the grocery store so that we didn't buy them out before the next one of us had a chance to shop.

I grimaced initially at the thought of making my own baby food. It sounded like a lot of work that would require a tremendous amount of time—something I'm short on to begin with. My neighbor, Krisi, was doing it for her son and insisted it was the easiest thing on earth, so I thought I'd give it a try. She was right. It is incredibly easy and does not take nearly as much time as you might imagine. You simply have to be efficient about it (and at this point, you're bound to be a world-class expert on efficiency). The first thing to do if you want to go this route is get a food mill—not one of the mini food mills sold at baby stores—you need a *real* food mill. Plus, when you've finished making baby food with it, you can use it to make pasta sauces from the tomatoes you grow in your garden—you know, in your spare time. The only other necessities are a food processor, a steamer basket, freezer bags, and ice trays—preferably the kind with angled cubes so you can stack the trays without sinking one tray into the one below it.

Barb thought I was nuts when I started making my own baby food. She gave it a try one day—I think mainly in an effort to prove me wrong—and within about three weeks, she was hooked. Of our entire group, I think only two of us did not turn ourselves into baby-food chefs once a week. And those two were happy as clams running to the grocery, loading their cart with baby food jars, and calling it a day. And, therefore, they should by all means have continued to do just that.

At the back of the book, I've included a section on making baby food. My girlfriends and I have done our best to take the guesswork out of whether to use the food processor or the food mill for particular foods. We've tried both.

Additionally, I highly recommend that you purchase (or borrow from your local library) *Super Baby Food,* by Ruth Yaron.

Ruth is a mother of twins herself, and this book is the most comprehensive I have seen on making your babies' food from the first bite through toddlerhood and beyond. She provides an enormous amount of information on why homemade baby food can be more beneficial (not to mention easier and less expensive) than its commercially prepared counterpart—and provides unmatchable variety at the same time. (Even I have grown tired of graham crackers and goldfish crackers, and I'm not even the one eating them!) Additionally, throughout her book Ruth addresses such challenges as the "picky eater" and the "seemingly endless eater," and even includes a month-by-month schedule for the introduction of foods in the first year (which includes *far* more dietary options than commercially prepared baby food).

If anything, during this three— to six- month period, you might start your babies on cereal, if advised by your doctor. Most start with rice cereal and then move to oatmeal and barley. I started with rice, but Henry was so constipated that even after starting him on prunes before cereal so that we could mix it with the cereal, he wasn't able to process it. We moved him (and hence, Jack as well) to oatmeal. (You want to see me crazy? Have me make one bowl of oatmeal and one bowl of rice cereal twice a day *and* remember who is supposed to get which!)

The best thing to do, as long as one of your babies is not sick, is to make up one or two bowls of cereal or other food, get one spoon, and just go back and forth. Honestly, if one kid is sick, he's probably already passed the germs to the other one, but to make myself feel like a decent, caring mother, I would use separate bowls and spoons if the boys were under the weather. In the beginning, it's easiest to feed one baby his cereal at breakfast time and the other after the first has finished, or feed the other baby his cereal for lunch or dinner. While they are learning to eat off of a spoon, it will be difficult to feed them both in the same sitting. And if you have two bowls . . . well . . . forget it. You'll be putting one bowl down to get the other bowl and they will both be protesting—one because he sees you feeding his sister and the other because she has this mouthful of food and doesn't know what to do with it! (Reserve the use of two bowls and two spoons for those times when a baby is clearly sick.)

With all foods, make sure that you feed the babies a single food for four or five days before moving on. Once you know that they can tolerate a food, you can combine it with a new one because then, if they have a reaction, you know it is the newest food that has caused it. I tried to keep my boys on the same schedule with new foods. However, Henry had prunes before Jack (due to the constipation issues) and just to be sure I didn't forget who had had what, I kept a little sticky note on the inside of my cabinet that listed which foods each baby had successfully tried.

WHAT'S GOING ON?

Another day, another new development. During the first year, so many new things will happen that there will be days when you don't know whether to think, "Hey, this is cool, something new!" or "Good Lord, could we *please* get some semblance of a stable routine in this house?" There are more than a few things that could occur, or begin to occur, during this three— to six-month period.

Important Things to Keep in Mind Regarding Development

- The guidelines provided by books on infant development are just that—guidelines. If your babies are not following the "standard" pattern of development, do not panic. Close the book and check with your pediatrician. There are many full-term babies who do not follow the standard pattern of development and even more premature babies who do not.

- There is a wide range of what is considered normal timing for any developmental milestone. Your friend's babies might do something at the early end of normal and your babies might do something at the later end, but they are both normal.

- Try as hard as possible not to compare your babies' development to that of your friends' babies, whether they, too, are multiples, or whether they are singletons. All babies are different and they are going to develop at their own pace. You may find that your friend's baby is rolling over at seven months and yours is not. However, do a little more talking and you may learn that your baby says, "Mama," while your friend's baby doesn't even seem to know who "Mama" is!

- Babies develop new skills quickly and usually at the most embarrassing time. My girlfriend Sonya was at the doctor for her boys' nine-month appointment swearing up, down, left, right, and center that her boys would not move at all and had no desire to crawl. As she was explaining this, the doctor sort of started laughing and Sonya turned to see her son using his heels to go backward on the table. Similarly, my friend Mollie was concerned because at nine months, her boys would not sit unassisted to save themselves. The doctor told her that at ten and a half months, if they were not sitting, they would discuss a plan of action. Two days later, the boys were sitting unassisted for thirty minutes at a time. The lesson is: Don't fear that because your babies are not doing something today, it means that they still won't have mastered it two weeks from now. They get motivation and skill quickly.

TEETHING

Every time my daughter cried, from the moment she was born, practically, until she actually had a full set of teeth, people would say, "Oh, she must be teething." They also said this because she drooled like crazy from the beginning. But that tooth never arrived. Same thing with my sons. They would cry and drool and drool and cry some more, and everyone would say they were teething, but nothing. Now, I do know that teeth bother babies long before you actually see those pearly whites. They hurt as they are coming up through the gums. Somehow, I doubt it took eight months for them to come up through the gums once they started their ascent, but I'm not a dentist. Barb, however, is a dental hygienist and I did call her probably sixteen times too many asking (as if she had a crystal ball handy), "Well, today it looks like thus and such. Do you think he'll get the tooth today?"

Honestly, just when you finally have some sense of a schedule, and your babies have slept all through the night for, say, two nights, they will suddenly regress—because they really are teething! They will wake up crying and/or will not go to bed easily. They may cry while drinking their bottles. Don't worry, it's just the universe keeping you on your toes and making sure you don't get too comfortable. After all, you are not allowed to do that until they turn one, remember? Most of us were sure that our babies' teeth were coming up a little and then going back down *over* and *over* until they would finally come in, only to have the peace interrupted for the next tooth that decided, that day, to begin its trek to daylight.

Tylenol works wonders for teething, especially right before bedtime, which is when most babies seem to be bothered most by the discomfort. My pediatrician does not recommend using topical anesthetics to relieve teething pain, but Barb swears by using just the slightest bit of baby Orajel right before bedtime. Her girls' teeth didn't bother them enough to wake them up at night, but they did bother them enough to prevent them from falling asleep. The Orajel took the edge off enough that they could drift off. I was always paranoid about overmedicating my boys, but after awhile, you just learn what behavior is normal and what is "off," and when it's off, you almost develop a sixth sense that it's their teeth (especially after that first one comes in and you can say with confidence that your child actually has teeth under his gums somewhere!).

ROLLING OVER

The sight of one or both of your babies rolling over is your first indication that times are a-changin'. It is so exciting to see one of your babies roll over for the first time. Pretty soon, he'll start on one end of the room and end up at the other end just by rolling his way across to get to something. So, when you see it happening, grab the video camera and then be prepared just to keep shooting that baby lying flat on her back because all babies know when they are expected to perform and are rarely willing to comply.

GET ME OUT OF THIS HOUSE
(WITH THE BABIES)!

Sometime during the three— to six-month period, you are going to wake up and say, "I have *got* to get out of this house." Your comfort with the babies' immune systems will be higher and if not, your lack of comfort staring at your walls will propel you to call the pediatrician and beg him or her to tell you that it is fine for all of you to run to the mall, the bank, or the park.

One of the best things to do first is something easy. Pick somewhere you can leave in a hurry if you have to (not the grocery store when you are trying to buy a week's worth of groceries). My first outing was to the mall (remember that early-on proclamation that I would *never* take all three kids shopping?). I had all three kids and it went beautifully—or maybe I just have selective memory. Try to time your babies' bottles simultaneously and leave directly after they eat so you have a few hours. Because you are trying to get them on a schedule as well, this is the perfect opportunity to get out and put them in the position where they cannot sleep or eat for awhile (though usually at this age, if they really need it, they can still sleep fairly well in the stroller). If they are awake, they will likely be distracted enough by the unfamiliar scenery that they won't have time to think they are hungry. As time goes by, work your way up the errand ladder. Within a couple of months, Barb could successfully complete about six errands in a row with her girls.

Solutions to Getting Out and About

Grocery Store
While your babies are still in infant carriers, put one in his carrier in the cart's front seat and one in the big part of the cart. If you are not getting too many things, you can probably fit groceries around the kid in the bigger part of the cart. If you are getting a lot of things, do what Mollie does and pull another cart behind you. I am, unfortunately, not coordinated enough for this option. Another idea is to put one baby in his car seat in the cart's front seat and carry the other baby in a front-pack carrier. This allows you all the room of the cart for groceries. Should you have a toddler with you as well, you might try one of those fun little carts with the car in front. When we tried this approach, Grace rode in the car part, one baby stayed in his car seat in the front of the cart, and I carried the other baby in a front-pack carrier. It should be noted that I did this only once, but I did get all my groceries purchased that day. As soon as the babies get older and are no longer in their infant car seats, you can sit one in the cart's front seat, put the other either in a front-pack carrier (if you can still carry her that way), or put her in a baby backpack. Sonya has been doing this and says it works great for her. Some forward-thinking establishments actually have carts with tandem front seats. I have become a very loyal patron of those establishments. Key to your success: Make sure all the grocery necessities are at the top of the list and shop for those first. Once you've gotten those, if all is still going well, move on to the other items on the list.

Sam's Club, Costco, BJ's, and other warehouse establishments
Put the babies in their stroller (a side-by-side stroller is undoubtedly not going to work for this excursion) and pull a cart behind you. Another option I discovered when I got to

one such store and realized I did not have my stroller in the trunk—sit both babies together (minus infant car seats) in the cart's front seat. Now, pay attention. You put their backs to the sides of the seat and put the right foot of the baby on your left through the slot and the left foot of the baby on your right through the slot. Their opposing legs just bend up next to each other in the seat. This did not work too well for me until the boys were about ten months old and were sitting up extremely well, and it only works for about thirty minutes at a time, but necessity is the mother of invention and this was my invention on that particular day.

Target and other quick stops
These are the perfect places to shop with your babies in their stroller. Lots of times, you are only browsing or picking up an item or two, which you can easily carry while pushing your stroller with your other hand. If you will be buying a lot of items, pull a cart behind you. Or, try putting both babies in the front seat of the cart if they are strong enough, and use the bigger part of the cart to hold your purchases.

Mall
The stroller is obviously your best bet here. A recommendation: Have a front-back double stroller for this trip. I tried using my double jogging stroller for about six months when I finally decided I was tired of not being able to get through Baby Gap with any ease whatsoever. I broke down and bought the front-back double stroller. I've said it before, but honestly, it was the best purchase I have made since the boys were born.

GET ME OUT OF THIS HOUSE (WITHOUT THE BABIES)!

It is at about this point that you might want to look into getting a sitter or two now and then if you don't have family in the area who can help out. I know it is daunting to try to find one person—let alone two—with whom you feel comfortable leaving your little angels. The cost of this arrangement can be more daunting still. Let me remind you of one important thing: Right about now, the cost of a sitter you are comfortable with will more than likely be cheaper than the cost of a one-hour session with a reputable therapist.

Additionally, many of my girlfriends' greatest fear is not that they won't make it through the day, but that when the day is over, and more specifically, when the next 5,000 days are over, they and their spouses will look at one another and say, "Who are you?" It is important to schedule little dates now and then even if it is just to walk around Target or go to McDonald's for an inexpensive burger and fries. Even a walk around the block can restore some of your energy and give you and your spouse an opportunity to talk about the day and life in general without the constant interruption of a baby in need.

As for dinners out, the time when the babies are still in their infant car seats is a great one for taking them to a local, family-friendly restaurant. If you are worried about the mass of people and germs, you are not alone. Try a restaurant where you order at a counter and then pick your table. The crowd at establishments like this is often minimal, especially early in the evening, as is the noise. You can eat at your own pace and leave when you need to. Truth be told, this probably works best if you do not have a toddler with you as well. At times, David and I could simply not justify the cost and hectic nature of going out to dinner. However, when the boys were ten months old, we did go to a local grill with all three kids and it went relatively well. The kids all shared pasta, and David and I even finished our entire meals (though we had major heartburn afterward because we were eating so quickly, sure that someone would have a meltdown at any moment). As the babies get older, they will enjoy more and more just watching all the people around them. And the people around them will be so enthralled with them (as you have undoubtedly already learned) that they will make faces at them and otherwise entertain them while you eat. You may have to address those folks who think your babies are public property and come over to touch them, but in the grand scheme of things, it is worth it to get out. Another option, if it is the right time of year, is to pack a picnic and head to a local park or other nice spot to eat. The point is to get out and spend some time together as a family.

A WAIST IS A TERRIBLE THING TO MIND

I remember when my obstetrician came into my room at the hospital to give me my discharge instructions. After I got a huge laugh out of the "no intercourse for six weeks" segment of his lecture, I got serious because he mentioned that most women who have twins come to their six-week appointment weighing less than they did before they got pregnant. As I stared down at my still seven-month-pregnant-looking stomach, I thought, "Could that be true?" No. It is not true. I mean, it may be true for some women out there who have the metabolism of a two year old, but for the general female population, I do not believe it is true. And frankly, the women for whom it is true are not my friends because it makes me frantic just to look at them. So, when I went in for that six-week appointment, having lost only twenty pounds (I was sure I had lost that in the delivery room alone), I was dumbfounded and confused.

Here is the bottom line: It took you nearly nine months to put the weight on, and it will take you about that long to take it off. But, you *will* take it off. I remember commenting to my mom one day that I really needed to exercise because my cholesterol was higher than it should have been, and she said, "Liz, I think you get plenty of exercise. It may not be for thirty minutes straight, but it's there." And she was right. Think about all the time you spend going up and down stairs, carrying between six and forty-five pounds (I am known, on occasion, not to feel like going up the steps more than once and simply carry up both boys, who weigh twenty-three pounds each, at the same time). You constantly get up and down out of chairs, you bend over and pick up babies, you shake bottles, you clean spots on the floor . . . Need I go on? This is all exercise! And the kicker—if you're eating three solid meals a day, you are my hero. I remember one week when the boys were about ten months old, we had our house on the market and I felt a bit ill. David asked what I had eaten recently and I remarked that in my short-term memory, there had been about six cupcakes and three or four Cokes. Maybe a piece of bread. That kind of limited food consumption does not breed weight gain. Unfortunately, it does not breed energy or good health either. Because both are highly valuable, try to eat high-energy, nutritious foods. Foods that can be eaten with one hand are highly underrated. Sliced turkey, cheese, and fruit were some of my favorites. Be *sure* you are taking a multi-vitamin each day. I have heard that even people who eat well should take one to ensure that they are getting all the nutrients that their bodies need. Because I don't have time to eat well, I *really* need that vitamin!

I would have loved to eat better all along, but truthfully, during that first year, I was so tired by 5:00 in the afternoon that I just didn't have it in me to cook a nice meal most nights. Also, by the time David got home, it was too *late* to cook a nice meal. I have included a large number of recipes in the back of this book that are easy to prepare—quick and with few ingredients—that can keep you "eating healthy" without taking up too much time or energy. This list was generated as members of our little sorority would call each other and ask, "What did you have for dinner tonight?" and, occasionally, say "Oh, that was a good idea!" I wish I had had this kind of a recipe list as a resource from the beginning. Another thing I wish I had had from the beginning: that great crockpot cookbook!

As for a workout routine, if you feel you need one, do what you can to fit in what makes you feel good. Barb was on the elliptical machine (I still don't know what one of those even looks like) every morning at 6:30 once her girls hit four months of age. I wanted to kill her. Mollie signed up at the YMCA when her boys were nine months old and put them in the nursery there while she did aerobics or the treadmill. I am still justifying to myself that all the exercise I get going up and down the stairs is adequate because I hate to do formal exercise.

While you *will* lose the weight, your body will more than likely never be the same. I can again fit into all my old clothes, but I will never, *ever* don a bikini again. I seem to have grown some extra skin on my belly that has no desire to go away. Some call it "twin skin." I call it my "war flab." Mollie calls it the "duffel bag" that is forever with her. While we would all love for it to vanish, it provides a memory of all those months we spent carrying the babies (small consolation, I know). Now, some say that a tummy tuck is the way to go. Maybe, but I don't have $4,000 sitting around, and I don't have three weeks to lie in bed and recover. Therefore, I have just resigned myself to the "no bikini" rule and called it a day on the tummy issues.

One little secret from this group: low-rise jeans and pants. Now, I had hips prior to getting pregnant so you can only imagine those hips after carrying and delivering nearly twelve pounds of babies. I would have been the first to state that there was *no way* you would catch me in low-rise *anything*! However, someone dared me to try it, just for the heck of it, and I have always had trouble refusing a good dare. I remember standing in that dressing room and staring at myself in disbelief. I looked. I hesitantly turned around and looked at my backside in the mirror. I repeated that exercise about ten more times just to be sure I wasn't so tired that I was hallucinating. My final conclusion: They really do work! Now, let me clarify that I am not talking about the *ultra*-low-rise pants. Those do not work on anyone who requires more than size zero pants, and most certainly not on someone who has been pregnant. The basic low-rise pants are sufficient. They make your rear look smaller, your hips *feel* smaller, and your body feel altogether thinner. Why? Because that "war flab" is no longer hanging over the waistband of the pants like a ball of dough waiting to be kneaded! An added benefit: Several of my friends believe that low-rise jeans are a godsend if you delivered by Cesarean Section because they don't rub as uncomfortably on the scar as their higher-rise counterparts.

Another secret: resale shops. OK, don't go crazy. I am not suggesting that you go to resale shops where everything is a mess and you are lucky if you find a pair of pants without six holes and two major stains. As I discovered, there are resale shops that are unbelievably nice. We have one nearby that specializes in high-end merchandise in fantastic shape. They require that all the clothing they buy (and then resell) arrives cleaned, pressed, and on a hanger. If there is so much as a smudge or an area that even looks like it might tear, they will not accept it.

I found this store to be invaluable during those months when I was "shrinking," but not yet into my pre-pregnancy clothes. It made no sense to go out and buy new clothes at that point—clothes that I knew I would (hopefully) be too small for in six weeks—but yet, my self-esteem was really taking a beating by my continuing to wear maternity clothes when the boys were already four months old. I found some unbelievable deals (I mean really, five dollars for a pair of J. Crew jeans in like-new condition—low-rise, of course!?). I was so impressed that I continue to shop there today, especially when I have an event to go to for which I have nothing appropriate to wear, yet I know that the next time I will have an opportunity to wear such an outfit, it's likely to be long out of style.

So now, I dare *you*. Check out low-rise pants and upscale resale shops in your area that carry clothing for adults. You might be thrilled with what you find!

CHILDPROOFING

You are probably saying to yourself, "Childproof? My babies aren't even rolling over. Why would I need to childproof now?" Well, my friend, because your babies will be rolling over before you know it and at that point, you will be too busy chasing them to have time to childproof. There are some things that are very easy to do quickly to provide *basic* childproofing. The rest you can do as you see the need, depending on your children's desires to explore things that should be off-limits. Here goes:

Early Basics

- Put outlet plugs in all outlets.

- Remove all doorstoppers that are the two-piece coil with a rubber bumper on the end. Babies are notorious for taking off that rubber piece and choking on it.

- Purchase a fireplace bumper pad if you have a raised fireplace hearth. Because no one has designed a fancy, aesthetically pleasing bumper pad, don't feel the need to put it up until at least one of the babies is heading for the hearth. It's better to have it around for when that day comes, however, just so you are prepared. And, on the off-chance that your babies do what Jack did and just crawl over and peel the thing off the fireplace every chance they get, I recommend a gate that can be assembled in a variety of shapes, such as a circle or arc. They are often called Supergates or Superyards. Shaped as an arc, it will prevent admission to the entire fireplace area.

- Get all cords off the floor. This will probably mean removing lamps from end tables and possibly moving floor lamps. Non-electrical wire, such as speaker wire, can be threaded under the carpet, but electrical wire cannot.

- Put cabinet locks on all lower cabinets, especially in bathrooms. If medicine is stored in those cabinets, get a tackle box, put the medicine in it, and lock the box with a combination lock. You can never be too safe about keeping medication out of children's reach. As a side note, I did leave one cabinet in the kitchen unlocked and store all of my Tupperware in it. It gives the babies access to one cabinet so they do not feel utterly and completely restricted, and the Tupperware will often entertain them for up to an hour or so. You may choose to actually *put* a lock on this cabinet if your babies are like Barb's girls. They enjoyed the Tupperware so much that they would get it out and push it back and forth across the hardwood floor, making a horribly high-pitched noise akin to running one's fingernails down a chalkboard. In the process, this game began to destroy her hardwood. As my boys approach thirteen months, I, too, am considering locking the cabinet, as their favorite pastime is letting one crawl inside the cabinet while the other closes the door on him, relegating him to total darkness until he screams so loud that his relatives in Nebraska can hear him.

Next Level of Childproofing

You will need to be prepared to do the following soon, if not now:

- Install gates at the top and bottom of your stairs. Also handy are gates that can be used to keep the babies in a particular room to play should you wish to clean adjacent rooms, cook, or be otherwise occupied without worrying where they are or what they are into.

- Research toilet locks. I discovered the beauty of toilet locks the day I found Jack splashing about in our toilet. It took him about eight seconds to get in there while I was changing Henry's diaper. I have been told that toilet locks have a tendency not to come off easily or completely when you are finished with them, so at a minimum, get into the habit of keeping your toilet lids down and the bathroom doors closed.

FIVE

6-12 Months:

Halfway There and Counting!

TOP TEN PRAYERS FOR THIS PHASE

10. When you turn one year old, please weigh at least twenty pounds so that we can turn these car seats around.
9. Please grant me one adult conversation per day.
8. Please provide me with a new and exciting indoor activity to do tomorrow. It's winter and it's freezing.
7. Please let my hairdresser have an opening soon. I barely recognize myself!
6. Please make all that crying part of my dream. Keep trying.
5. Please let there be clean clothes in the closet and edible food in the refrigerator when I wake up in the morning.
4. Let the person on the other end of that ringing phone be calling to tell me that despite the chaos in this house at this moment, I'm the most wonderful, talented mother in all of the world!
3. Please keep the food *on* the tray!

2. Please help these children to understand that "no" and "time-out" correlate, *before* they get to the time-out spot and have a fit.

1. It is 3:00 in the morning. If there is a God in heaven, please help that baby to understand (and soon) that he is *not hungry!*

Great news—you're halfway there! Even better news—the toughest half is behind you. I promise, the next six months will go by so quickly you will hardly believe it. Of course, you will still have challenges and will be almost constantly developing and refining your strategies for dealing with said challenges, but you will feel oh-so-much more capable of dealing with them because, for starters, you will be operating (most of the time) off of a good night's sleep! You will also be more comfortable with your babies' flexibility, schedules, and personalities. You will know what you can get away with and what you cannot.

By this point, your babies should be on a fairly set schedule. This schedule is likely to change just a tad over the next six months as the babies possibly give up (every so often) their morning naps, further define when and how much they will eat, and transition almost entirely to table foods.

If you are still fighting the pounds you put on during your pregnancy, this is the period when you will shed them. The reason? You will be moving constantly. Why? Because your babies will be. During this six-month period, they will undoubtedly learn to crawl and may start cruising around furniture or, if you're really being put to the test, start walking. At eleven months, Jack was ready to take off for the Boston Marathon, but Henry wasn't even crawling. The pediatrician had Henry continue physical therapy once a week, but I decided that not only would he do it when he was ready, the universe was looking out for me because to have two children moving as fast as Jack moved at the time would have had me in a constant sweat. It is during this period that you will definitely want to acquire gates and begin to set boundaries for your babies as far as what they are allowed and not allowed to play with, in, on, or under.

WHAT PART OF "NO" DO THESE CHILDREN NOT UNDERSTAND?

Your babies will start to understand the word "No" sometime during this time frame. Whether they will obey it is another story entirely. Jack absolutely understood what "No" meant early on. As he was attempting to scale the fireplace, I would calmly say, "Jack, no no." He would turn his head, slowly look at me, give me a mischievous smile, turn back, and continue what he was doing. It was almost as though he wanted to see how many times I'd say "No" before getting up and dragging myself to the other side of the room to move him (which only kept him away from that fireplace for about twenty seconds). It is important that your children understand "No," but it is equally important that they not be forced to hear it all the time. They will start to wonder what they can explore and the word "No" will begin to lose its meaning if used too often.

Try to remove as many things in your home as you can that pose an unsafe distraction to your babies. Use "No" when necessary to keep them from climbing on fireplaces, pulling over chairs, or attempting to play with outlets (even though they are covered). It is important that you not make your home resemble a padded box because your babies need to learn to respect boundaries. Otherwise, when you go to a friend's house—one who has all her beautiful Lladros out on prominent display—and you say "No" to your child as he's getting ready to grab the biggest and most expensive one, he won't understand what you're saying (or potentially that you are talking to him specifically) and you'll find yourself the proud owner of a (broken) Lladro.

I have a whole room that is the designated toy room. It's technically a dining room, but we don't have the time or the energy to entertain more than this family, so we converted it into the toy room. There is nothing in there that the babies may not play with.

I can gate them in or just put them there to play and not worry about what they are into. It is safe for them to explore, and it allows me freedom from constant in-their-face supervision. They can develop their independence by playing alone or with each other, and I can cook dinner or straighten up the rest of the downstairs (a temporary thing, I can assure you).

One suggestion my pediatrician gave me was to start using time-outs with the boys when they would not obey the word "No." I never found that time-outs worked particularly well with Grace, but one day Barb called and said she was giving them a go with Olivia and Kambria, and so I decided to join her; after all, I would never want one of my girlfriends to go through any part of this alone!

Our big struggle, and the one for which I began using time-outs, was the TV. The boys were obsessed with it. They would push all the buttons, turn it on and off, and/or turn the volume up as high as it would go (undoubtedly so that they could make a case for the fact that they couldn't hear me as I said "No"). It drove Grace crazy because the TV continued to flip from *Sesame Street* to the devotional channel, to blaring static, but never back to *Sesame Street*. It drove *me* crazy because they were not listening to my simple request that they not play with the TV. Playing with the television is virtually the only in-house activity to which I say "No." Everything else is either locked shut or put away. The boys have hundreds of toys with which to entertain themselves and I would argue that most of them are far more interesting than a television, but what do I know? Clearly, a thirty year old's definition of fun differs a wee bit from that of a pair of one year olds.

My first approach was to copy Mollie's self-devised solution to the TV problem. She had Gary go to Home Depot and buy a piece of pre-cut Plexiglas (with rounded edges) the size of the control panel on their TV. They attached the Plexiglas to the control panel area with Velcro. Rather ingenious! I didn't have Plexiglas and I needed a solution immediately, so I cut out some cardboard and affixed *it* to the TV with Velcro. Within seconds, the boys were at the TV together ripping it off. Super. Glad I could provide them with something to do together, as a team, that did not involve wrestling or biting, but I quickly got over my joy.

From that point on, each time one of the boys would go to play with the TV, I would say, "No. We don't play with the TV." They would usually look at me and smile, but didn't move. I would then say, "No playing with the TV or you'll have to go to time-out." They would smile and continue to play with the TV. So, to time-out they would go. I set up a Pack 'n Play in our dining room (our empty dining room). There were no toys in the room, nothing in the Pack 'n Play, and once in it, the kid could not see anyone else in the house unless someone walked past the room.

I would usually leave them there for just one minute or so. (The times they ended up there together were interesting.) It took many trips to the Pack 'n Play, but after awhile they got it. Jack got it more slowly than Henry, but he got it nonetheless. There are still days when they "forget" the no-TV rule, but it takes far fewer trips to the designated time-out zone before they remember and find something else with which to entertain themselves.

Barb was actually carting each of her girls to a time-out zone upstairs each time she did something she was not allowed to do. As I've mentioned, Barb is in incredible shape. Despite moving all day long, I am not. Or maybe I just hate breathing heavily and sweating. Either way, I refused to go up and down those steps over and over again each time I had to utilize the time-out zone. Besides, for quite some time, each time Jack got out of the time-out zone, he inevitably went right back to doing what got him put in time-out in the first place—and therefore, had to go back (a good reason not to designate the time-out spot upstairs).

CAN WE PLEASE GET SOME VARIETY IN THE MENU?

During this period, you will go from feeding almost entirely baby foods (commercially prepared or homemade) to feeding more and more table foods. This is a good thing and a messy thing. I was so excited for the days when my boys could eat finger foods *by themselves.* However, I quickly learned that although you may have that fifteen-minute break while they are eating, you will then lose fifteen (sometimes twenty) minutes as you clean up the floor, the trays, and the babies. So, you can take the time to spoon-feed them forever and keep the dining area and the kids clean, or you can let them have at it and just pencil in "cleanup time" into your mental daily schedule.

We all struggled with what foods to introduce during this period. Obviously, you will start with easy-to-pick-up, easy-to-chew, easy-to-swallow foods. You will then get bored with them (and so will the babies). At about eleven months, you will be calling everyone you know with a small child and asking what on earth they feed them because you just feel positively abusive continuing to give them Cream of Wheat every morning and afternoon.

Some good foods to introduce during this period, as you feel your babies are ready, are:

- Cheerios
- Pieces of bread
- Diced peaches/pears
- Soft green beans
- Black beans
- Pasta
- Nutri-Grain bars (broken up)

For a whole *slew* of additional options, refer to Ruth Yaron's *Super Baby Food.* Be prepared for the fact that picking up this food and putting it into their mouths will take a bit of time. Jack went right at it, hand over fist, but Henry would not even touch it for weeks. Once he got over that, he would pick it up and just hold it. A few weeks later, he would pick it up and put it in his mouth, but would not let go of it, so he'd just suck on it until it was utterly obliterated. Finally, he learned. And I got down on my knees and thanked God.

As your babies get more skilled with foods, you can introduce the more complicated (and real, everyday) stuff. Some suggestions:

- Pancakes (Make a whole batch and freeze the leftovers. Just thaw them on subsequent days as needed.)
- Grilled cheese (Cut sandwiches into bite-size pieces.)
- Cheese sandwiches (ungrilled)
- Cubed turkey, ham, or cheese
- Cottage cheese
- Yogurt
- Macaroni and cheese (We spoon-feed this one!)
- Lasagna (if you are having a particularly brave day)

Because the digestive system is not fully mature at birth, Dr. Liberty recommends avoiding peanut butter, nuts of any kind, eggs, fish, and citrus fruits during the first year and maybe longer—depending on the individual child. Check with your pediatrician regarding any other foods you should avoid due to family allergies or other predispositions to possible allergies. These might include berries or whole wheat. The list will likely be small (unless you are Mollie, whose husband we call "bubble boy," poor thing has so many allergies), so you can use this time to experiment and see what your babies enjoy.

Also, be sure to avoid foods that may pose a choking hazard to children less than three years of age. These include, but are not limited to:

- Raisins and other dried fruit
- Nuts
- Hot dogs
- Popcorn
- Chips
- Pretzels
- Grapes
- Hard candy
- Gum
- Jelly beans
- Whole corn kernels

One issue we all struggled with during this period of food experimentation was whether or not our babies were getting enough to eat. We had learned that two jars of commercial baby food or four frozen homemade baby food cubes were enough, but once we started throwing all that diced stuff out there, were they eating until they were satisfied? Was their mid-afternoon meltdown a sign of extreme fatigue or extreme hunger? When I asked Dr. Liberty about this, she commented that regular visits to the pediatrician's office to watch the child's growth are important. Every infant is different. Some infants do very well with solids at six months, for example, and others may be slower to start. She cautions parents against forcing a spoon or any foods into their child's mouth. If the infant opens his or her mouth for food, seems interested and content, she recommends following those cues. Most toddlers will exhibit a decrease in appetite at around twelve to fifteen months because their growth and calorie needs are changing. Dr. Liberty recommends offering small (diced) bits of food with a good variety. Do not fill a toddler plate because it usually just overwhelms children of this age and they do not eat well. It is not uncommon for toddlers to eat only a few bites of each thing served. She also cautions parents against giving toddlers frequent snacks between meals that may suppress their appetites. This includes juice. The high sugar content is an appetite-killer and juice (even fruit juice) is not very nutritious. Toddlers may need three to five small meals per day. Keep meals/snacks nutritious. Most children under age three do not eat for any reason other than hunger (unlike their mothers who often do it out of boredom alone). If your babies are cranky and accepting food, they are likely hungry.

Additionally, families should eat together when possible because children learn their eating habits from their parents. Now, I practically had a coronary after hearing this. Our kitchen table only seated four. The boys would normally eat before David got home, and Grace often ended up eating by herself at the table as I got the boys ready for bed. I would then down the infamous Rice Krispies dinner around 8:00PM while David complained about how hungry he was. Needless to say, we felt horrible for Grace and knew the dinner hour provided a great opportunity to talk as a family, so we invested in a larger table. (Jack and Henry are often excused at this stage of the game from the formal dinner ritual.)

RIDDING THE CUPBOARD OF ALL THOSE BOTTLES

At this age, you will also want to start introducing sippy cups to your babies. They may want nothing to do with them for some time. With my daughter, we just ended up having to go cold turkey the day after her first birthday. My pediatrician warned me that she might not consume any liquids for an entire day to try to make us feel bad enough to give back her bottle. It was a long day, and she did a lot of screaming. But by the next day, she took that sippy cup and never looked back.

With the boys, I started offering sippy cups of water during their feedings when they were about seven months old. Many times, they would just touch them. Other times, they would throw them on the floor. I wasn't worried about whether they drank from them or not, I just wanted the boys to get used to them. I'd start trying to offer them sips out of the cups and Henry would drink from it, but only if I held it; Jack just chewed on it. Neither option was portending long-term success, but patience is the key here. By eleven months, both babies would drink out of the sippy cups—when they wanted to—and I knew that when we had to throw the bottles out, they would be thirsty and would use the cups.

Many people buy a certain brand of sippy cups and when their babies don't get it right away, worry that it is the spout or that the particular brand of cup is too hard to suck from, and they wonder if the solution is to try another sippy cup. I have been one of those people. I own at least one of every brand and style of sippy cup on the market—handles, no handles, spill-proof spout, no spill-proof spout, rounded cup, straighter cup, you name it. My advice to you is this: If you are concerned, try *one* other brand of sippy cup. If they get it with that one, while it may be coincidence, pat yourself on the back and proclaim that you knew it all along. If they don't get it, do *not* go buy another variety. Before you know it, you will have every brand on your cupboard shelf and more than likely, your babies will take to none of them. Or they will take to a newer one, but give them the other brands and I can guarantee they will take to those, too—they just figured how to drink from it, that's all!

NEW CAR SEATS—AGAIN!

Sometime during this period, you will switch from the infant car seats (if that's what you started with) to the convertible rear-facing/front-facing car seats. Remember, your babies *must* face backward until they are one year old *and* twenty pounds. The main reason is that an infant's neck is not strong enough to handle a head-on collision, and the damage to the developing brain if the head were to forcibly snap forward could be severe. Twenty pounds is recommended for proper fit of the harness in the larger car seats. I know that getting your babies in and out of those backward-facing car seats, especially if they are in the back row of a van or large SUV, is a nightmare that often prompts vivid dreams of weekly visits to a licensed massage therapist, but it is worth it for their safety.

There are so many car seats out there to choose from. Our recommendation is that you find one that not only faces backward, but also has a tether strap to further secure the seat in your vehicle. These tethers are amazing and will make your car seat fit so tightly in your car that you will feel like it is part of the vehicle.

Installing these seats backwards is no small feat. If you try and try and sweat and sweat and still are not comfortable with the fit, call your local police station like you did with the infant car seats, and ask to make an appointment to have your car seat installed. Note that while not required, the car seat checkers who do on-site inspections at stores such as Babies "R" Us often want you to have your babies with you so that they can verify how you are buckling your baby in, which is as important as how tightly your car seat is installed.

THE INCOME POTENTIAL OF A GARAGE SALE

There will come a point during the first year when you will suddenly realize how much stuff you have accumulated that is no longer being used: infant car seats, infant clothes, swings, bouncy seats, Boppy pillows, the list goes on and on. If you plan to have other children, in fact, if you think there is even the most remote possibility that you might want to have another child, I would encourage you to find a nice spot somewhere in the recesses of your basement to stow all this stuff until you might need it again. If, on the other hand, you are like me and have declared that only by an act of God will you ever bear children again, there are easy (and profitable) ways to rid yourself of all of this stuff.

The first, which we have all found to be the most profitable, is eBay. Now, early on, I encouraged you to hold onto the original boxes that the gear came in so that if you chose to sell it in this way, you would have an easier time packing it than if you had to start from scratch. If you did not heed my advice or for some other reason are no longer in possession of those boxes, it's OK. You can improvise, or you can decide to rid yourself of those bigger items via other means. eBay is a great place to sell baby equipment. It goes fast, and it almost always goes more profitably than it would in a garage sale. I have no idea why. With shipping, folks are many times paying close to what they would pay for the item new, but when you are making the dollars and not spending them, I say don't spend a lot of time questioning the actions of perfect strangers.

Another method for getting rid of all that stuff is to hold a garage sale. Mollie and I did just that when our babies were about nine months old. Garage sales are great for getting rid of baby clothes because to photograph and list all those clothes on eBay really won't pay off financially in the end. Most folks buying clothing on eBay are looking for items advertised as NWT. Garage sales are also a great way to get rid of bigger items. If you advertise "baby" in the garage sale ad, people will come running. If you advertise "mother of twins" or "multiple mothers of twins," as we did, you will have an even better turnout. I was able to rid my basement of an infant car seat and coordinating stroller through this sale that I never would have even attempted to sell on eBay because for one thing, I would have no idea how to package it and for another, it would have cost about $200 to ship.

PLAYING TOGETHER (OR NOT!)

It will be within this six-to twelve-month timeframe that your babies will likely start to interact more and more. Be prepared; it may not be in the most positive way. That need not matter. The key is that they know the other exists and if they have fun battering each other, at least they are entertaining one another, albeit perhaps temporarily.

The first real interaction Jack and Henry had was not so nice. Henry was ultra-dependent on his pacifiers, and Jack seemed to know this, so at eight months of age, he would reach through the crib slats into Henry's crib, steal the pacifier right out of Henry's mouth, and chew on it. As you can imagine, Henry had the biggest fit you have ever seen, and it always required intervention from David or me. As time went on, they would enjoy playing tug-of-war with toys and talking to each other more and more. Seeing multiples begin to interact is one of the greatest joys of raising them.

GETTING AWAY: THE ROAD TRIP

There will likely come a time during this period when you will think to yourself, "I don't care where we go, but we have *got* to get out of this town for a day or two." You will then likely debate whether the inconvenience of loading up everyone and everything is worth it to get those days in a different locale. More possibly, you won't even stop to think about the logistics because you will be so in need of simply getting away!

Believe me, this is doable. Holly and Paul headed out one Friday to go camping for the weekend with their ten-month-old triplets. I thought they had lost their minds. Not only did they pack up the necessities—bottles, formula, food, clothes—they packed two exersaucers, bouncy seats, maybe even a swing, I don't know. They had a blast. They were so relieved to be away from home that they didn't even think about the inconvenience. And they swear that the girls were so excited to be in a new environment that they slept better than they ever had and seemed happier than they had been in some time.

When our boys were about nine months old, we headed to my parents' house for Memorial Day weekend. We followed Mollie and Gary, who were headed to Mollie's parents' house. Their drive was about nine hours. Ours was nearly fourteen! We followed each other for about the first six, talking back and forth on walkie-talkies, and then split to go north and south respectively. It was a great, although short, weekend. However, just the excitement of getting away made the long drive and frequent stops well worth it. And since we drove through the night, David and I had more successive hours just to talk about whatever we wanted than we had since the boys were born. (By the way, if the drive to your final destination is a long one, driving through the night is a very good idea. If you can manage to stay awake, you can log several hours of driving time without having to stop to feed or change someone.)

You need not go on a long trip to get the feeling of being away. Find a neat town within two or three hours and head there for the weekend. Preferably, find somewhere with a kid-friendly atmosphere, family restaurants, and places to walk. It does not work well to go somewhere with a largely adult, antiquing crowd (and mostly antique shops to boot), for instance.

THE JOY OF SELF-SUFFICIENCY

I swear, the greatest joy I have felt in the last year—next to realizing I had just slept for eight hours without interruption—was the sight of Jack holding his own bottle. If the neighbors had seen the happy dance I did upon noticing this feat, they surely would have concluded that they were living next to a complete weirdo. He accomplished this about two weeks before Henry and about four weeks *after* Olivia and Kambria. (I had to ask Barb not to mention that the girls were eating because I knew that meant that they were eating while she was doing something else, whereas in my house, I was a slave to the boys' need for me to hold their bottles for them.) It felt like instant freedom. I thought to myself, imagine the possibilities here: I can mix and give them their bottles at 5:00AM without having to sit there for thirty minutes holding them. I can hand them their bottles, change their diapers as they drink, and then go back to bed. (Luckily, my boys didn't fall asleep while drinking their bottles and just threw them out of their cribs when they were finished. I know I'll pay for this luxury somewhere down the line, but right now I'm not worried about it.) I can have them drink their bottles as I make dinner. I can give them bottles in their car seats as I am driving and not be forced to stop in the parking lot of some grocery store, squeeze my understandably huge hips between those car seats, and give my arms the workout of their lives holding the bottles up while they drink more slowly than molasses flows in winter. If your babies are not yet able to hold their own bottles, be patient. This is a skill that usually emerges quite suddenly, so who knows, it could happen tomorrow!

HAS THE SUPPLY OF GIFT CLOTHES FINALLY RUN OUT?

During Holly's triplets' first year of life, they were dressed in the most adorable, nearly matching outfits you have ever seen. Each time I would comment on them, Holly would indicate that the outfits had been a gift. I started wondering when those were going to run out (and I don't think they have yet!). However, at some point they will, and you will be faced with purchasing not just one adorable pair of wide-wale corduroys or tights with multi-colored butterflies all over, but two (or more). This can start to feel prohibitive in a hurry. You'll find yourself saying over and over again, "If I only had to buy one of these, I could justify it, but *two?*" One note about this: Chances are, if you did have to buy only one, you would still be trying to decide if you could justify it. I learned this going from having one baby to having two. It's all perspective. I shudder to remember the days when I thought having one infant who slept eighteen hours a day was "challenging" and had "interrupted my routine."

There are some practical ways to get around this clothes-buying dilemma. One is garage-sale shopping. I swore up and down when I had Grace that I would not buy my kids' clothes at garage sales, but you would not believe how nice some garage-sale clothes can be! In more affluent areas, people won't even attempt to sell clothes that are not in great shape. I have really lucked out, and I can say with all sincerity that some of my favorite clothing items for my sons this winter came straight from some trendy mom's high-quality garage sale.

Another option is second-hand children's shops (yes, here I go again with an endorsement for second-hand shops). You have to pick and choose among these stores, as some don't require the same quality in the clothes that they buy and resell, but there is one near my house and I know of others elsewhere that demand nearly new condition when buying from sellers. The only downside of second-hand stores is that oftentimes, by the time the store has added its markup to the price required by the seller, it's actually cheaper to hit a good sale at the Baby Gap. However, I have lucked out repeatedly at second-hand stores and been thrilled with my finds.

Another fabulous solution we've devised within our little sorority is borrowing clothes from each other when our kids are not wearing the same sizes. Mollie's boys are five weeks younger than Jack and Henry, but are also about eight pounds lighter. They are still in size 6-12 months clothes while Jack and Henry wear size 12-18 months. So, all gifts that Mollie received for the winter in a 12-18 month size are currently hanging in my closet and as my kids outgrow them, hers will be growing into them. Since we live in the Midwest, it will undoubtedly still be snowing in April, and her kids will still get plenty of use out of the items. (So, all of you who bought 12-18 month winter outfits for Mollie's children need not feel bad; you've clothed four kids instead of two!)

Be sure to inquire at stores as to whether they offer a twin discount. Many outlet stores even offer a ten percent discount above and beyond their already low prices. A few stores are gracious enough to offer this discount not only to parents of twins, but to grandparents of twins as well. Some establishments offer a discount on anything except sale merchandise. It would appear that certain stores seem to have determined they are actually *losing* money by giving discounts to mothers of twins because there are so many twins out there. Therefore, such stores have revamped their multiples discount to apply only to triplets and beyond. Regardless, it's always worth checking.

WALKING

This is an activity that may or may not begin to surface by the time your kids reach twelve months of age. I froze stiff when I looked into my dining room (a.k.a. the toy room) and saw Jack standing up in the middle of the room with no support whatsoever. I whispered to myself over and over, "Sit down, Jack. Just slowly . . . sit . . . down." Granted, he was thirteen months old when this occurred, but my point is that if it has not happened yet, it's probably on the horizon, so just prepare yourself.

Now, some of the positives of your children learning to walk (since every stranger you bump into will be proclaiming the negatives): They will be able to walk on short outings, they will soon be able to climb into the car and maybe even into their car seats, they will be able to walk where you need them to go (even though they are probably already crawling there, but hey, I'm just trying to point out the positives here).

I REALLY THINK I NEED TO GO BACK TO WORK

Many new moms of twins return to work either for financial reasons, or because their job is part of what defines them, and they are uncomfortable parting with that aspect of their life. If you plan to go back to work after having your babies, be sure to research your childcare options early on. I know several people who were shocked to find that some reputable daycare facilities in their area had a waitlist of up to six months. If you plan to explore the nanny or au pair option, careful planning is again the key. Many nanny or au pair placement agencies require several months to process an application, conduct interviews, and establish final placement. It would be wise to get this process under way before you are nearing the end of your pregnancy because with two babies on the way, you never really know exactly when the end will be!

Not every woman has to return to work immediately after having her babies. Some are fortunate enough to be able to stay at home with their babies if they so choose. However, if you opt to be a stay-at-home mom, "I think I need to go back to work" is a phrase that you are likely to utter more than a few times during this time period. The reason? You're tired of a few things.

Possible Reasons For Wanting to Return to Work

- You're exhausted. You will be convinced (and possibly right) that it would be easier physically and mentally to be a garbage man dumping everyone's fifty-pound trashcans or a construction worker building eighty-story buildings all day than doing what you are doing.

- You're tired of not having adults to converse with all day long. You're concerned that one day, you might find yourself having a professional conversation with someone in that high-pitched I'm-talking-to-a-baby voice.

- You're tired of hearing about the delicious meal your husband had for lunch.

- You're convinced you are getting dumber by the second for not having to use your intellect very often anymore. (I have a stack of *New York Times* crossword puzzles—granted, in a drawer—that I have pledged to do just to keep my brain fine-tuned.)

- You have convinced yourself that your kids are getting sick of your presence and are never going to obey the word "No," regardless of how nicely you say it.

Any of that sound familiar? I contemplated returning to work no fewer than 197 times before the boys turned one. Sometimes I was serious and other times, not so serious. Luckily, I have a husband who is incredibly supportive and told me that if I needed or wanted to go back to work, he would stand behind me 100 percent. Usually, what squelched my desire to return to corporate America rather quickly was my lack of desire to find someone to care for my kids while I was already in the throes of doing the job myself. With three children, I could be making $60,000 a year and practically losing money to have them in a formal daycare. It was also important to me to keep them in their own environment. That meant finding a nanny. I just never got to the point where I was able to start the tedious process of finding one we were happy with. Plus, in order to pay the costs to search for and then employ a nanny, I had to have a well-paying job. In order to work that job, I had to have a nanny. Even as a mother of multiples, there were too many logistics to coordinate at once. As you can see, there's great benefit in researching childcare options early.

When the boys were nearly one year old, my friend Stephanie, who had babysat for the boys early on and then left her full-time job to get her Masters in Education, offered to quit her part-time job and work for me three days a week as a nanny. I was so elated I thought I would burst. I knew Stephanie well, she is fabulous with my kids, and my kids love her. What more could you ask for in a nanny? I sent out résumés left and right. Now, I did not just send them out blindly. I sent them out in response to job postings on popular job-posting Internet sites. These were positions for which the companies were supposedly looking to hire. However, even though some of the positions might have been a stretch, given my background, many of them seemed a perfect fit—at least close enough to get a phone call! But nothing happened. I never heard from anyone. After spending a few hours wondering how I had become so completely invaluable, I decided that perhaps I simply wasn't meant to return to work at that time. In the course of this whole multiples thing, you find yourself having to turn a lot of it over to fate. It takes some of the burden off you, anyway. I thought, *Maybe—even though I'm ready to pull my hair out—the place I will be of most value at this point is here in this house with these children.* If the right opportunity presented itself, I would still consider it, but it would have to be suitable for me and for my family. Such an opportunity has not yet arrived. Therefore, I'm going to continue to relish the opportunity to help these kids grow and develop and learn to say, "Please."

My friends Sonya, Jean, and Holly all work full-time. I think that more than wanting or needing the money, they enjoy working. I remember watching an interview with Cindy Crawford shortly after she had her first child. She was asked whether it bothered her that she had received a fair amount of criticism for returning to work after her son was born. She responded that she was a person who *had* to work to some degree. She said she had cut back considerably, but in order to be a good mother to her son, she had to do something other than just stay at home with him all day long. It was how she stayed sane and focused. I think that is highly respectable. Once they have children, women are sometimes criticized for working if they don't need to for financial reasons. But the bottom line is: You have to do what you have to do to be the best mom you can be. And if that includes working two or three or five days a week, part-time or full-time, then that is what you have to do. At the end of the day, both you and your children will be better for it.

So, if you start to feel the "I've gotta go back bug", explore it. See what your options are. If an appealing opportunity presents itself, that give it a try. What do you have to lose? I know several women who work at their local department store two nights and one weekend day a week in order to get away and earn some extra spending money. They love it! There are definitely options beyond working 100 hours per week. You must simply determine what will work best for you and for your family and find something that will accommodate those parameters.

SIX

Happy Birthday!

You did it! Wasn't so bad, was it? When our boys turned one, people asked over and over, "Can you believe they are a year old already?" I did not know how to answer that question. Time certainly does fly, but when I thought back to the day they were born, it seemed like ten years earlier. Each day can feel like a lifetime, but each year feels like a day. As I finish this book, Grace is three and a half years old and the boys are nearing fifteen months. The boys wrestle with each other. They steal from each other. They push each other. They cannot go to sleep at night unless the other is in his crib within eyesight. Jack calls Henry "Bobba." The other day, Jack went over and sat on Henry's lap (and Henry had a complete fit). They are beginning to speak their own language (and I shudder to think what they are saying about me). And the best is yet to come—potty training, preschool, drivers' licenses, college . . .

So, as I close, I have several wishes for you: May you feel blessed every day. May you eat a good, warm meal at least once a week. May you have an amazing group of supportive friends who make you laugh when you need to most. I can promise you one thing: Our sorority is with you every diaper, bottle, and step of the way.

I NEED YOUR HELP!

I am creating two new books for mothers of twins. The first, *Cupboard Full of Chocolate: Morsels of Wisdom and Humor for Mothers of Twins* will contain humorous and/or serious pieces of advice and words of wisdom for soon-to-be and new mothers of twins. The second, *One Stork, Two Babies: Stories Behind the Blessings*, will contain heartwarming stories related to the pregnancy with, delivery of, and life with twins.

I would be flattered to receive your contributions to these works. Please make your submissions via my website, www.elizabethlyons.com, for inclusion. You will be able to include, if you desire, your name and information about your children (names, ages, birth date). All personal information is optional; providing it will neither ensure nor prohibit inclusion of your contribution in the published works.

I look forward to reading your submissions!

APPENDIX A

Making Your Own Baby Food

As I mentioned earlier, making your own baby food could not be easier. With a toddler running around in addition to my twins, I would be the first to admit it had it been too much; remember, I'm the one who had to return the hospital-grade breast pump after the first rental month because I could not find time to pump. So, if I am saying you can do this, you can do this!

To reiterate, there is nothing wrong with commercial baby food, in my opinion. It's convenient and the serving sizes are prepared ahead of time. But it's expensive, and as I learned after making my own food, it has limitations when it comes to variety and the combinations the manufacturers have chosen. I mean, plums and tapioca? Enough said. Additionally, commercially prepared baby food often contains more water, starch, and sugar than homemade baby food.

There are some simple supplies you should have on hand before you begin:

- Food processor
- Food mill

- Steamer basket
- Ice cube trays
- Sandwich bags
- Gallon-size freezer bags

HOW TO MAKE BABY FOOD

Preliminaries

Some simple rules regarding food safety should be followed when making your own baby food:

- Be sure to wash your hands and your tools thoroughly before making your babies' food to ensure that no germs or other contaminants are introduced into the food.

- Do not let cooked food come into contact with raw food in order to reduce the likelihood of bacterial contamination.

- Do not let baby food sit at room temperature for more than two hours. After this point, bacteria can begin to grow. Refrigerate or freeze the food as soon as possible after preparing it.

Step-by-Step

1. Wash hands and equipment well with hot, soapy water.
2. Wash fruits and vegetables and remove skin, if desired, and seeds. I left skins on occasionally after scrubbing them really well. If you have a good food mill, the skins will either be left behind or will become so ground up that your babies won't even notice they are there.
3. Bake, boil, or steam food until tender.
4. Use a food mill, blender, food processor, or fork to mash food until smooth.

5. If necessary, add liquid (water, formula, or breast milk) to thin out thick foods. I also believe that adding some formula or breast milk to food you will freeze helps it to thaw with a creamier texture as opposed to a more freeze-dried texture.

6. Pour food you will use in the next twenty-four hours into a bowl in the refrigerator; put the remainder into ice cube trays. Cover filled ice cube trays with plastic wrap and put them in the freezer for a day or so until the cubes are frozen. Pop the cubes out and put them into a large, labeled, and dated freezer bag.

7. When you want to use cubes from the freezer, simply put the number you wish to thaw in a bowl in the refrigerator or microwave them for a few seconds. You do not need the food to be too warm; it only needs to be at about room temperature. If using the microwave, be sure to stir the food *very* well to eliminate hot spots. Also, test the temperature of the food before offering it to your babies.

BABY FOOD RECIPES: THE BASICS

*NOTE: These foods are listed in approximately the order in which most of us offered them to our babies. There is no right or wrong approach regarding the order you choose. It is a commonly held belief that it is a good idea to offer vegetables before fruits because the fruits will give your babies a taste for sweeter foods; they may then not be interested in the vegetables. I know people who have started with fruits, however, and done just fine.

Storage Times

Food	In Refrigerator	In Freezer
Fruits and Vegetables	1-2 days	2 months
Meats or Egg Yolks	1 day	2 months
Meat and Vegetable Combo	1-2 days	2 months

FRUITS

Peaches

Remove pit and slice peaches into wedges. Steam peaches until they are extremely soft. (Steaming helps to keep the vitamins in the food; if you boil the fruit, you will lose more of the vitamins in the water.) Use a food mill to purée them. The skins will either be ground up so finely into the peach mixture that you will not notice them, or they will stay behind in the food mill. The food will likely be so watery that you will not need to add any breast milk or formula to it. If you need to add some liquid, use the liquid that is in the bottom of the steamer. It has plenty of vitamins from the peaches. Put the peaches in ice cube trays and freeze.

Pears

Follow instructions above.

Plums

Follow instructions above.

Bananas

I usually waited until the bananas were extremely ripe and then mashed them with a fork to the desired consistency. When combining bananas with another fruit or vegetable, simply mash the desired quantity and stir in with the other food before transferring the food into ice cube trays. Remember not to combine bananas with other foods until you know the baby can tolerate the food to which you are adding the bananas.

VEGETABLES

Green Beans

We found frozen green beans to be the easiest to use. We also found them (along with peas) to be the least desirable to the babies. Steam the green beans until they are extremely soft and then purée them in a food processor. If your babies don't seem to take to the green beans, try mixing them with a sweeter vegetable that you have already tried, such as sweet potatoes or squash, or mix them with a fruit once you have ensured that your babies tolerate the fruit.

Peas

Again, frozen works best here. Steam the peas until they are very soft, then purée them in a food processor. As with green beans, if your babies don't seem to like peas, try mixing them with sweet potatoes or squash, or mix them with a fruit once you have ensured that your babies tolerate the fruit.

Sweet Potatoes

Pierce four to five sweet potatoes with the tines of a fork and microwave them for approximately 25 minutes on high. Alternatively, you can bake them in the oven at 375°F for an hour to an hour and a half. Scoop out the flesh and blend it, along with an ounce or two or formula or breast milk, in a food processor. Continue to add breast milk or formula until it is creamy. Spoon into ice cube trays and freeze.

Squash

Cut several butternut squash in half. (We tried a variety of squash and found that butternut works best.) There is no need to add butter or brown sugar to the squash, unless, of course, you plan to eat one yourself for dinner! The squash is plenty sweet on its own for the babies' tastes. Cook the squash at 350°F for 45 minutes to an hour, until the flesh is soft. Scoop out the flesh and blend it, along with an ounce or two or formula or breast milk, in a food processor. Continue to add breast milk or formula until it is creamy. Spoon into ice cube trays and freeze.

MEATS

Truth be told, none of us actually made our own puréed meat. The texture (and smell) of it did not particularly agree with the babies or frankly, with the adults! Once our babies were old enough (around eight or nine months of age), we would offer shredded meat or meat diced into small pieces. Success was also found through putting chicken breasts or a roast in the crockpot, cooking it for six to eight hours, and then shredding it. You can easily add flavor to the meat this way, which makes it far more appealing.

Many of us found that regardless of being shredded, diced, or puréed, our babies wanted nothing to do with meats until they were closer to fourteen months old. To ensure that they were getting adequate protein until that time, we offered them cheese, beans, yogurt, and other protein-rich foods. Ruth Yaron shares some great ideas in her book for protein alternatives such as tofu or tahini.

Once you know that your babies will tolerate a variety of the above foods, combine them! I made batches of plums and sweet potatoes, or bananas and pears, or a combination of three or more. The more foods you combine, the larger the batch will be, which is helpful if you are running low on food and need to make a big batch of *something*. It's easier to make a big batch of pears, bananas, and green beans than it is to make separate batches of each of those and combine them later.

If your babies don't enjoy green beans or peas as much as you would like, make a batch of pears and add a small amount of green beans or peas. The sweetness of the fruit may persuade them to eat it and they will still be getting a healthy serving of vegetables as well, without really knowing it.

APPENDIX B

Quick, Tasty Recipes for the First Months and Beyond

O h, how I wish there had been an appendix like this in one of the books I read when I was pregnant with my boys. Heck, I wish there were a whole *book* out there devoted to easy, quick, tasty meals for new moms. Therefore, I'm going to take two good ideas and combine them into this little appendix. That way, you do not need to go out and buy too many more books (I will suggest that you get one or two on crockpot cooking). Hopefully, this reference will keep you well nourished and prevent your getting sick of handfuls of Cheerios and peanut butter on a spoon. For those recipes that make more than you need, freeze the extra! Most will leave you with at least a little bit left over for the next day's lunch.

As mentioned above as well as early on in this book, I strongly recommend getting your hands on a cookbook that is devoted to recipes for the crockpot. Some that I've found helpful are: the *Biggest Book of Slow Cooker Recipes*, by Better Homes and Gardens (this book even includes a chapter on five-ingredient recipes and one on one-dish dinners!), and *The Ultimate Slow Cooker Cookbook*, by Carol Heding Munson. The recipes are delicious and many of them do not require that you chop vegetables for six hours straight. Another bonus: You simply throw your ingredients into the crockpot, turn the thing on, and go do what you have to do for the next six to eight hours. The house will fill with the inviting scent of good food and when you are ready to eat it, it's hot and waiting! Should you get ready to serve yourself and someone starts wailing, you just put that lid back on and know that whenever you get to it, it will still be warm. The crockpot is the greatest invention ever. Bon appétit!!

NOTE: All recipes serve approximately four people.

SOUPS, SALADS, AND SIDES

Fast Vegetable Soup

1 can chicken broth
2 cans vegetable broth
1 small can tomato paste
Salt, pepper, and thyme to taste
1 pkg. frozen vegetables (of your choice)
8 oz. alphabet pasta (or other pasta)

In a pot, combine all ingredients except vegetables and pasta. Bring to a boil. Add vegetables. Cook for 10-13 minutes or until tender. Add pasta. Cook until tender. Season to taste. Serve with quick-bake rolls such as Pillsbury Dinner Rolls.

Potato Leek Soup

3 leeks, chopped
1 T. butter
1 tsp. salt
1/4 tsp. celery salt
1/8 tsp. pepper
1 cup potatoes, boiled and mashed

2 cups milk with 1 chicken bouillon cube or 1 cup milk w/1 cup chicken stock

First, wash the leeks to remove sand and dirt. When chopping leeks, chop from the bottom (discarding root end) to the top until you come to the part of the leek that fans out. Sauté leeks in butter until tender. Add the rest of the ingredients and simmer for 15 minutes. You can thicken the soup with instant potatoes, if necessary. Serve with quick-bake rolls, such as Pillsbury Dinner Rolls.

Apple Salad

Keep a bowl of this in the fridge for when you need something quick to eat. The fact that the word "salad" is in the title will make you feel good about it!

1 can chunk pineapple
2 cups mini marshmallows
1 egg
1 T. flour
1 ½ T. Vinegar
1 (10 oz.) container of Cool Whip
2 large apples, unpeeled and chopped
½ cup sugar

Drain pineapple, saving juice. Mix pineapple and marshmallow together. Refrigerate overnight. In a saucepan, beat egg and mix with pineapple juice. Add flour, vinegar and sugar to egg mixture. Cook over medium heat until thick, stirring constantly. Refrigerate overnight. The next day, combine Cool Whip with egg mixture. Add apples. Finally, add the pineapple/marshmallow mixture.

Mandarin Jello Salad

Another great one to have in the fridge to snack on!
1 6 oz. package orange JELL-O
3 cups hot water
1 pt. orange sherbet
1 bag mini marshmallows.
1 (12 oz.) can mandarin oranges, drained
1 (12 oz.) can crushed pineapple, drained

In a 9x13 pan, dissolve jello in hot water. Add sherbet. Let partially set (for maybe an hour or so). Add mandarin oranges and pineapple. Top with marshmallows. Chill until completely set (will take approximately three more hours).

Pasta Salad

To provide those all-important carbs!

1 (16 oz.) package tri-color rotini pasta, cooked and drained
1 cup chicken, cooked and shredded
1 ½ cups cheddar cheese, cubed
¼ cup Italian dressing
1 red or green (or both!) pepper, cut into small pieces
Sliced olives (optional)

Combine all ingredients and refrigerate for approximately two hours to allow tastes to combine.

Creamed Potatoes and Peas

1 lb. new potatoes
10 oz. frozen peas
2 T. butter or margarine
1 T. chopped onion
2 T. flour
½ tsp. dill weed

1 ¼ tsp. salt
1/8 tsp. pepper
1 ½ cups milk

In a medium pan, boil unpeeled potatoes until tender. Drain. Peel potatoes, if desired. Set aside. In the same pan, cook peas as directed on package. Drain. Set aside. Melt butter in pan and cook onion until tender. Blend in flour, salt, pepper, and dill. Stir in milk. Stirring constantly, heat to boiling and thickened. Add potatoes and peas. Heat through.

Five-A-Day Salad

Romaine or Iceberg lettuce
Frozen or canned peas
Canned kidney beans
Cubed cheese
Red, green, or yellow pepper
Ranch dressing

Put lettuce on a plate. Place heaping scoops of all other ingredients, except dressing, around the sides and middle of the lettuce. Top with dressing.

Hash Brown Potatoes

You can add cubed ham to this and have a delicious main dish.

2 lb. bag frozen hash brown potatoes
1 tsp. salt
¼ tsp. pepper
1 cup onion, finely chopped
1 can cream of chicken soup
1 pt. sour cream
1 (10 oz.) bag cheddar cheese, shredded
2 cups crushed corn flakes
½ cup butter or margarine, melted

Thaw potatoes. Mix salt, pepper, onions, soup, sour cream, and cheese with potatoes. Put in a 3-qt casserole dish. Top with corn flakes and butter/margarine. Bake at 350°F for one hour.

MAIN MEALS

French Toast Casserole

1 loaf French bread
3 eggs
3 cups milk
4 tsp. sugar
¾ tsp. salt
1 T. vanilla
2 T. butter, cut into pieces
Cinnamon

Grease a 9x13 inch glass baking dish. Slice French bread 1" thick. Arrange the bread on the bottom of the dish. By hand, beat together eggs, milk, sugar, salt, and vanilla. Pour evenly over bread. Cover and refrigerate overnight. Before baking, put pats of butter on top of bread slices and sprinkle with ground cinnamon. Bake at 350°F for 45-60 minutes.

Quick Quiche

1 ½ cups Monterey Jack cheese, shredded
½ cup cheddar cheese, shredded
3 eggs
1 cup Half and Half
1 jar marinated artichoke hearts, drained and chopped
3 slices bacon, cooked and crumbled
1 frozen piecrust

Bake piecrust as directed on package. In a bowl, add eggs and Half and Half. Mix well. Add cheese, artichoke hearts, and bacon. Pour into cooled piecrust. Bake at 350°F for 45 minutes.

Spaghetti Squares

8 oz. thin spaghetti
1 egg, slightly beaten
¼ cup milk
1 (15 ½ oz.) jar spaghetti sauce
4 oz. pepperoni, sliced
8 oz. mozzarella cheese, shredded
Parmesan cheese, grated

Cook spaghetti until al dente. Drain. Beat egg with milk and combine with spaghetti. Place in a buttered 9x13 inch pan. Pour spaghetti on top. Sprinkle with pepperoni, mozzarella cheese, and Parmesan cheese. Bake in a preheated oven at 350°F for 25 minutes. Cut into squares.

Pasta, White Bean, and Tomato Stew

2 T. olive oil
1 onion, finely chopped
3 cloves garlic, minced
3 cups canned tomatoes, chopped
1 cup small dry navy beans
5 cups chicken broth
5 oz. dry pasta (any variety)

Soak and cook beans according to package directions. Set aside. Sauté onion and garlic in olive oil. Add tomatoes, salt, and pepper to taste. Simmer for 20 minutes. Add cooked beans and broth. Simmer covered for 20 minutes. Add pasta and cook until done.

Delectable Bean Burritos

1 (15 oz.) can black beans
1 (15 oz.) can corn
1 cup salsa
4 12-inch tortillas
2 cups Monterey Jack cheese, shredded
1 cup sour cream

Put beans and corn in a saucepan and warm until heated through. Microwave each tortilla on a plate for 10 seconds on high. Place two or three spoonfuls of bean/corn mixture onto each tortilla. Top with cheese. Roll up tortillas and microwave individually for 30 seconds on high. Top with sour cream and salsa.

Chicken Enchiladas

8 soft flour tortillas
4 cooked chicken breasts
2 cups mozzerella cheese, shredded
1 cup salsa
2 cups lettuce, shredded

Spray a rectangular cake pan with a non-stick cooking spray. Shred the cooked chicken. Mix the chicken and most of the cheese together. Place some of the chicken/cheese mixture into each tortilla and roll up. Put the rolled tortillas seam-side down in the pan so that they do not come unrolled during baking. Bake at 350°F for 15 minutes to allow cheese to melt. Sprinkle remaining cheese over top and return to oven until just browned. Serve with salsa and shredded lettuce on the side.

Chicken Wine Supper

4 boneless, skinless breasts of chicken
4 pats of butter

4 slices Swiss cheese
1 can cream of mushroom soup
1 cup white wine
Bread crumbs

In a baking pan, lay out the chicken breasts. Put a pat of butter on each. Then, lay one slice of Swiss cheese on each chicken breast. Spread soup over chicken. Pour wine over all. Sprinkle with bread crumbs. Bake at 350°F for one hour, uncovered. Serve with wild rice.

Crunchy Chicken Salad

This recipe is great to make on the weekend and munch on for lunch during the week.

5 cups chicken, cooked and cubed
1 lb. green grapes
1 cup celery, chopped
1 (10 oz.) can water chestnuts
1 cup slivered almonds
Dressing:
1 ½ cup mayonnaise
1 T. soy sauce
1 T. lemon juice
1 tsp. curry powder

In a large bowl, combine first five ingredients. Set aside. Mix dressing ingredients well. Pour over chicken mixture. Stir well. Chill for one hour and serve with crescent rolls.

Ground Turkey Meatballs

These are wonderful to bake and then freeze, especially if you have a toddler in the house. Once the babies are eating table food, meatballs are great to have prepared and frozen; they can be thawed and served in a flash.

1 1/2 lb. ground turkey
2 eggs
2 cups bread crumbs
1 cup milk
1 tsp. salt
1 cup chicken broth

Combine ingredients and shape into balls. Cook in pan, searing first on all sides. Add chicken broth and simmer until fully cooked through. Let cool in refrigerator and then freeze.

INDEX

Printed in the United States
22399LVS00002B/11